Prayer for use before the daily reading

Heavenly Father,
Guide my thoughts,
Forgive my distractions,
Help me to listen to your Word,
In Jesus name.
Amen.

Prayer for use after the daily reading

Loving Lord,
Help me to live this day,
Consecrated to you,
Seeking to serve,
Open to your Spirit,
Conscious of your love.
Amen.

LENT WITH SAINT JOHN'S GOSPEL

John Mann

Lent with Saint John's Gospel

A SERIES OF REFLECTIONS ON VERSES FROM
SAINT JOHN'S GOSPEL ARRANGED TO BE READ
DAILY THROUGHOUT LENT

the columba press

First published in 2014 by
the columba press
55ᴀ Spruce Avenue, Stillorgan Industrial Park,
Blackrock, Co. Dublin

Layout and cover design by The Columba Press
Printed by CPI Antony Rowe Ltd

ISBN 978 1 78218 130 9

Thanks

I would like to thank my wife, Helen, for her encouragement and many helpful suggestions. I am also grateful to the Literature Committee of the Church of Ireland for its support, and to all the staff at the Columba Press that have made this book happen.

Contents

Introduction

Buying a Lent book is a positive thing to do, showing the intent to mark the days based on our Lord's forty days and forty nights in the wilderness, as a measure of our belief that discipleship begins with preparation and self-examination. Many people reading these words will be in the habit of locating and studying a Lent book every year, either on their own or in the company of others. I do hope that the days of this penitential season that lead us to the Cross, and to Easter, are a source of encouragement and joy and that we are ever more ready to follow Jesus.

There are forty-seven daily reflections in this book. Lent is, in fact, forty-six days long because the days of penitence should not include Sundays, and there are six of them in Lent. I have included Easter Day as well, for the sake of completion, so that makes forty-seven in all. The texts that I have taken for each day are all short, so reading around each verse is necessary in order to appreciate the context of the passage as a whole – even when the verse is a very familiar one – otherwise the reflections may seem disjointed. The book requires one to have a copy of St John's Gospel to hand, to read it at least every few days; better still, to reread the relevant chapter every day. In truth, the book is designed with that intent in mind.

Lent is a time that leads us through the dust and ashes of its beginning, experienced against the backdrop of John the Baptist's exciting and challenging ministry at the River Jordan, through the wilderness temptations of Jesus to the threatening pressure of the last few days of our Lord's earthly ministry – at least prior to his Resurrection. It is a season of the Christian Year in which we are encouraged to undertake some discipline – to 'give up something' or make a bit of an effort to go to church more often, be a better person, give something for the needs of others and try to take the whole of our discipleship more seriously. It is very easy to point to the deficiencies in a great deal that people attempt, especially in the area of denying ourselves our little luxuries, but even the more difficult striving to act in a more loving way, especially towards those we find it almost impossible to encounter. It is probably better to step back a pace and apply ourselves to the underlying desires and promptings of our day-to-day lives.

Herein lies the driving principle behind both the style and structure of this book. I felt that to create a focus around a particular daily theme – a well-tried and tested formula for a Lent book – takes some bettering. Some of the days do lead into each other, but mostly they are designed to stand alone. If you start and then miss a few days, don't worry; just pick it up again at any stage and carry on. I hope that this can be a gift from me to you. It comes with my prayers; I shall reread each day with you and look forward to that joy and privilege throughout Lent. It will be very special for me; I hope it is some help to you.

John Mann
Epiphany 2014

How do I use this book?

I have written these reflections with two main possibilities for use in mind: first, the individual wanting a daily thought throughout the course of Lent; second, the group, studying week by week, for the whole period. So I knew, from when I began, that the book needed to be split into days and into weeks, but then, there is always someone who wants to read a Lent book straight through in one sitting, so it required a coherent theme: what binds the whole is St John's Gospel. The daily reading is the chapter of the Gospel in which the text of the day is found; this is taken as the constant, so the daily and weekly thoughts are randomly built around this, rather than structure the book on themes that then require suitable texts to be found. On this basis, reading the relevant chapter each day, by the time you have finished Lent, you will have read St John's Gospel at least twice.

I have notionally divided the book into sections[1], for, potentially, five discussion group meetings; and it is also split into days – to last from Ash Wednesday to Easter Day. For each week, holding seven specific meditations, there naturally develop some specific thoughts linked to the Bible passages under consideration, raising issues of relevance to personal and home life, parish and community life and matters of a broader, more philosophical or ethical nature. Questions for discussion are easily constructed to meet your own needs, but I make some suggestions at the end of the book. I trust you will treat the whole of this offering as just headings for thought, just the scribble on the untidy side of a proper address; as a reminder that the original scripture is what is important, and it is addressed to you and, thankfully, also to me.

Section One

Ash Wednesday to Day 8
'The Challenge'

John the Baptist – The Desert – The Coming of
Jesus – Cana and the First Miracle – Nicodemus
and the Proclamation of a New Birth

Day 1 – Ash Wednesday
St John's Gospel, chapter 1 verse 23: 'He said, "I am
the voice of one crying in the wilderness."'

The voice of John the Baptist is what we are to hear; the sight of him may draw the eye of the imagination – not many are dressed in camel's hair and eat locusts and wild honey – but 'the voice' draws the mind into the same space that John occupies. That is crucial to the appreciation of what this powerful prophet is trying to say to all who will take the trouble to hear. 'The voice' may bring the vision of a talent show in our day, but for John's audience it was a throwback to the prophet Isaiah, one who spoke much of the release of humanity from the many things that constantly tend to bind and imprison.

At the beginning of Lent, on this first day, as we step into the desert with Jesus to face the temptations and trials of the journey of faith, there is a sense that to do so with the words of John the Baptist ringing in our ears, is the best of all introductions. There is an abrasive edge to John that it is good to experience. Some years ago I recall spending a few days with my family in the Burren. We walked over those amazing limestone pavements, peering down grikes and looking hard for the jewels of the area's flora, but we were left recognising the rough edge of the search for what is promised. Symbolic of this were the pink pads of our dog's feet – we were not aware, because of our strong shoes, that the poor animal had such sore paws.

The journey can be rough at times and insensitively we may shy away, once we realise the nature of our chosen path. People may not help with words such as, 'You've made your bed, you may lie on it!' – but the essential risk involved in seeking a life-changing Lent is also what generates the excitement; the sense of newness; freshness; tuning the ear to a voice coming to us from the wilderness; an abrasive voice, one to disquiet the calm and maybe, yes probably even, calm the disquieted!

John the Baptist is such a voice for all who seek to engage with the truth of the Gospel of Jesus Christ, who take the words of the New Testament and receive them in humility, rejoicing in the wrestling, being challenged in the gusts of the Holy Spirit as the voice of God is heard within, through the words written or spoken of others, that are like a magnet to pull us into a closer engagement with the scriptures. Susan Sontag, the American commentator on contemporary life until her death in 2004, paraphrased Goethe's words as 'Whatever doesn't kill me, makes me stronger'[2]. That is an especially abrasive way of beginning the desert journey, of hearing the voice of John and entering the wilderness with Jesus, but let us find the courage to step beyond the threshold of this season and feel the dust between our toes.

Day 2
St John's Gospel, chapter 1 verse 26: 'Among you stands one whom you do not know.'

The wilderness of Judea is not like the Sahara Desert. It is barren dust and rock rather than sand. The vegetation, such as it is, appears like a haze on the face of the ground, especially in the bright glare of the noontide sun. In the early morning, or late afternoon, the slanting light of the low sun picks up the contours of the undulating ground, in the shadows and bright facets of contrasting planes of vision. We are metaphorically in that wilderness on this second day of Lent, searching for our bearings, but John's comment is made at 'Bethany beyond the Jordan' (verse 28), where he was baptising. It is from this place[3] that the view across the Jordan towards Jericho takes in the mountainous region beyond, that is thought to be the area of the Judean wilderness in which Jesus spent the time of his temptation.

The Evangelist, St John, does not mention the temptations of Jesus, but is still leading us, at this point in the text of chapter 1, to consider the words of John the Baptist that are directly related to our Lord, 'Among you stands one whom you do not know.' The unknowable raising that spectre of that which is 'miss-able' is something that has concentrated the minds of Christians for centuries. The Baptist was pointing the way, but he needed to show that it is only with eyes open to what this extraordinary person is that the searchers are likely to spot him. The obvious, even the very needy, spontaneously reaching us through the moral observation of the socially conscious, can still miss the solution on offer.

Have you walked along Custom House Quay in Dublin and looked at the sculpture by Rowan Gillespie of the famine migrants to America? The ragged, drawn, bronze figures are spread over an area of the quay. It is a living, developing sculpture as others may add plaques to the horizontal perspective of the whole, linking the present day reflections and effects with the desperate memories of the past. It is a powerful image, showing the proximity of suffering within the reach of a trying remembrance. As I stood there a few weeks ago, a foreign tourist was attempting to capture this scattered collection of sculptures into what it is meant to be, one composite work of art that holds integrity of structure with a single vision of anticipated effect.

For me, that man reflected the state of many of us in the wilderness of early Lent; searching for bearings in the changing patterns of light, whist recognising that the one who is going to guide us is there before us, quietly standing in the midst, ready to lead us on.

Day 3
St John's Gospel, chapter 1 verse 29: 'Behold the Lamb of God, who takes away the sin of the world!'

'The voice', having intimated that his listeners are not recognising Jesus in the midst of the crowd, makes a stunning proclamation: 'Behold the Lamb of God, who takes away the sin of the world.' This verse, with verse 36, where 'Behold the Lamb of God' appears again, may refer us back to Isaiah 53 verse 7: 'He was oppressed, and he was afflicted, yet he opened not his mouth; like a lamb that is led to the slaughter, and like a sheep that before its shearers is dumb, so he opened not his mouth.' We have a few contrasts to be observed between Jesus and John the Baptist; one is the relative silence of Jesus at the early stage of his ministry (he returned to an almost silent mode of engagement towards the end, as we shall observe later) with the abrasive and didactic 'voice' of John the Baptist.

The contrast of silence and voice is apparent from the verse from Isaiah quoted above also. Is the role of the servant of God to be one of silence or proclamation? The easy answer to this is 'Sometimes one and sometimes the other!' However, first the servant is in the situation of 'listener'. This is the silence of attention, which is quite a different matter to the silence of Jesus, or the silence of the lamb. In this position, we understand the silence of the Lamb of God as projecting something in the nature of a control, that allows others to take the initiative. This needs to be somewhat unpacked. Later we will consider the silence of Jesus before Pilate and others, but at this early stage of the Gospel story, Jesus is the object of observation in the context of a strongly projected message from John the Baptist. This allows Jesus to build a persona in the minds of the followers of John, that both contrasts with him – and fulfils his ministry. John may envisage this in a supplanting way, in all humility and love, but the silence of Jesus may be understood as an approval too. This is a point to which it is worth returning in due course.

The use of silence in contrast is one that we may explore liturgically, though primarily silence when utilised in this way is for reflection, rather than effect. Nevertheless, the 'Great Silence', at the Eucharist can be envisaged as shaping a mirrored image of the taking, as well as a chance to observe what the receiving is for. In other words, that the flow of the inner life of the Spirit's activity within is both a contrast with the distracting clamour of the mind's chatter, but equally provides a starting point for the conscious awareness of the power of silence to announce, or even promote, the beginning of something important in our lives; perhaps a fresh understanding of the glory of God.

Day 4
St John's Gospel, chapter 1 verse 39: 'Come and see.'

He said to them, 'Come and see.' These words of Jesus are spoken to two of the disciples of John the Baptist in answer to their question, 'Rabbi, where are you staying?' In this testing first chapter of the Fourth Gospel, the nature of the person of Jesus, as much as the nature of the person of John the Baptist, is being teased out. Primarily, the chapter indicates this in the opening prologue, which mentions John as 'a man sent from God' and gives a deep theological explanation for the presence of Jesus amongst humanity at a particular time in history.

The explanation of the Incarnation is by no means an easy matter for us to connect with, familiar though the whole concept has become, and there is always the danger of under-estimating the full impact of the miracle of the Son of God becoming man. Christmas is the time at which these verses are read: 'In the beginning was the Word, and the Word was with God, and the Word was God.' The Christmas Gospel has a 'Come and see' urge to it. 'The true light that enlightens every man was coming into the world.' 'Come and see.' 'Yes, do!'

Four years ago, when I was Rector of St John's Malone, I reversed the traditional way of reading the nine lessons at the Christmas Carol service. I asked the Bishop to read the none-too-easy first lesson from Genesis; I, as Rector, read the second and we went right through in ascending order as is customary, with a ten-year-old child, Sarah, reading the Prologue to St John's Gospel. She read it beautifully, and set the whole place of the Incarnation where I believe Jesus would have it, in the simple fact of untrammelled human potential and frailty. The seeing is vital.

'Rabbi, where are you staying?' Indeed, where is Christ's dwelling? He is with humanity, truly; in the hearts and souls of those whose love for him; in drawing the searching desire of the vulnerable into the place of grace. 'Come and see' is the invitation to grapple with the mystery; the desert, the testing of Jesus and what it means to be baptised. That is enough for one day. These themes will come back in the days covered by this Lent book. 'Come and see' is the invitation, 'Stay and see' is the plea.

Four days concentrating on the first chapter of the Fourth Gospel is inadequate to absorb even a fraction of its riches. In Lent, as our eyes are turned to the desert, to a place of testing, and primarily to the person of Jesus Christ, the opening that St John the Evangelist provides for us, in terms of its introduction to his namesake, John the Baptist, and Jesus himself, inspires us to want more. So, after rereading chapter one, be ready to move on tomorrow!

Day 5 – The First Sunday of Lent
St John's Gospel, chapter 2 verse 3: 'The mother of Jesus said to him, "They have no wine."'

On this day the Gospel reading is, inevitably, an account of the temptations of Jesus. These do not appear in the Fourth Gospel, so we find ourselves in another preparation place for ministry – not the desert, but at a wedding. The contrast could not be greater. While we shall hear of Jesus being tempted to turn stones into bread (which he does not do) read in Church today, from Saint John we read of him being asked to produce wine (which he does). While his mother doesn't actually ask him to perform a miracle, she simply points out the problem, with the expectation that Jesus would be able to do something, as she adds (to the servants), 'Do whatever he tells you.'

Bread and wine are two of the things that we meet today, the very essence of sacramental communion, but not being introduced in a sacramental, or at least devotional, way. In both cases the reader is being asked to consider the lack – of bread in the wilderness and of wine at the wedding feast – and what the reaction of Jesus is to be. In the case of the temptations, the Evangelists explain that Jesus was being 'tempted of the devil'. The experience of the forty-day period of our Lord's testing, upon which Lent has been established, must have been related to the disciples later by Jesus, as he was in the wilderness alone. The very trial of his ministry was being worked out as each temptation was presented to our Lord and then banished, using the words of scripture and the voice of authority.

The lack of wine at the wedding feast is an entirely different matter. There had been wine and it had all been drunk. What Mary's particular concern was we do not know, but she must have, in some sense, felt the need to intervene and help to solve the problem that lay before the bridegroom, who was, eventually, being credited with keeping the best wine to the end – when guests, having already drunk a significant amount, may well not notice. Clearly, she had confidence in her son; that he understood what was needed and could fulfil it.

The fact that Jesus undertook this first miracle to create a situation of happiness at a wedding, and avoid embarrassment, we may either be puzzled by or look for some hidden meaning; some reason that goes beyond the meeting of a particular human need at a particular moment. Jesus resisted that temptation in the wilderness.

What appears to be of key importance is the context. In the wilderness Christ seemed to be testing his vocation, by the time of the Wedding at Cana, he knew what he had to do and how he was going to do it. He indicates that that time had not yet come, but nonetheless he was ready.

Day 6
St John's Gospel, chapter 2 verse 11: 'This, the first of his signs, Jesus did at Cana in Galilee, and manifested his glory; and his disciples believed in him.'

Yesterday, we considered the place of Christ's first miracle in relation to his temptations in the wilderness and how the beginning of his public ministry was being announced. Two characteristic words of St John's Gospel occur in the last verse, relating this miracle of turning water into wine, namely 'signs' and 'glory'. In the Fourth Gospel, miracles are described as 'signs' and the 'glory' of God is a frequent point of reference.

So it is that the consideration of our Lord's early days of public ministry, taking us as they do both to the desert (through the Synoptic Gospels) and to a wedding feast (in the Fourth Gospel), challenges us to consider how discipleship may be initiated and sustained. We are aware that Jesus was about thirty years of age at this time, indicating that preparation for Jesus involved living an 'ordinary' life for a long time – proportionately, a very long time, when seen against the average life expectancy of the day. That preparation must have included a substantial concentration on the scriptures and on prayer. This in itself is what we might expect, but also indicates that the path of part-time, patient study and training in the spiritual disciplines, whilst involved in a busy trade or other career or job, is not only possible, but perhaps even desirable.

I am now nearly twice the age that Jesus was, but I can picture how I felt at thirty and what sort of a lifestyle I was living. The 'signs' that made my view of the world coloured by the glory of God were around me always; our children were young and were themselves exploring, we were hard up and counting our pennies, but it was the competing demands on time that were an important part of the picture – as is the case for many young couples seeking to bring up a family and balance work, further study and scraping around for the odd new purchase in the home.

Within all of these things there was a sense that God was guiding and teaching us, through the many adventures that came our way. In themselves, there was nothing out of the ordinary, but miracles are frequently in the eye of the beholder, and, whilst I have always resisted a fatalist attitude to life – that somehow everything is predetermined and that even evil things happening to us are God's will – I do understand that there may be signs of God's glory across a wide range of demanding experiences. There is a lot of food for thought in this, as there is in why the servants drew wine from those stone jars rather than water!

Day 7
St John's Gospel, chapter 3 verse 4: 'Nicodemus said to him, "How can a man be born when he is old?"'

This surely stands as one of the great questions of life; it excites profound answers; it stirs the mind to miracle: 'How can a man be born when he is old?' Just sit back and contemplate the thought: 'In Christ all things can be made new!' I have always loved that concept of the day revealed as a microcosm of one's whole life, awaking in the morning as if born afresh, growing more weary as the day and its happenings absorb time and effort, finally in the declining hours, resting in the words of compline to the darkness of night, trustfully, seeking the arms of the Father, surrounded by the angelic presence, which seems more imminent, though was never absent from the beginning.

But, you will say, the answer of Jesus to Nicodemus is declaring more than that: 'Truly, truly, I say to you, unless one is born of water and the Spirit, he cannot enter the kingdom of God. That which is born of the flesh is flesh, and that which is born of the Spirit is spirit. Do not marvel that I said to you, "You must be born anew."' Jesus is instructing Nicodemus in the ways of salvation; in the life of the Spirit, rather than the prescribed demands of the law. That limitless life, that Jesus maintains through his own presence in the lives of those who find in him a friend and brother as well as a Lord and Master. The faith that is shown forth in the words and works of those whose lives are conforming to Christ, is also seeking the imitation of one whose steps are there to be followed. What is meant by this being born 'anew', 'from on high', or simply and most commonly rendered, 'You must be born again', has been, rather surprisingly, one of the causes of separation between Christians. But no matter, what we celebrate this day, in the presence of Nicodemus and Jesus, is a great meeting of minds on the profound mystery of the spiritual life.

Nicodemus draws the conversation to the physical and the impossibility of new birth in that physical sense, causing Jesus to develop the response as a dichotomy between the inner and the outer; between the body and the spirit. Within the popularity of Incarnational theology today, emphasising the 'presence' of the God-borne within the human-centred; the place of the holy/wholly spiritual within the earth bound, there is a little bell ringing, reminding us to be careful not to fudge theological distinctions. That said, the intention is to draw Nicodemus into a new life of service, which challenges him to consider the spiritual heart of all legitimate appeals to Christ. Nicodemus is doing this very thing. Whilst he seeks illumination, he gains the information he is searching for, to have his life changed radically by Christ. He may come by night, but he leaves as a child of the day, or so we may assume, as he becomes a disciple of Christ, whilst remaining a Pharisee. The light of which our Lord speaks is now clearly exposed.

Day 8
St John's Gospel, chapter 3 verse 30: 'He must increase, but I must decrease.'

The quality of John the Baptist as both one who went before, and ultimately a follower of, Jesus Christ has never been in doubt, but this comment, 'He must increase, but I must decrease,' perhaps beyond his many other striking pronouncements to his disciples and the crowds and others, is filled with what we would recognise as a Christian core. The natural human response would demand that John would be jealous of Jesus – just imagine Jacob, or Joseph or Jonah giving way to another in this way! John saw his role in a process determined by God that was both vital and limited.

This stirs another thought: Can we envisage leadership within the Church, that couples a prophetic message with built-in obsolescence? This is a surprisingly exciting thought and may have been practised in the Church without us realising it. That is a slightly tongue-in-cheek comment! Meant to be positive – but easily taken negatively, as if we place people with ability and wisdom in high office and then strip them of the opportunities that they had previously, to influence people at the grass roots. That is what seems to have happened to John the Baptist. He retained to the end his effect upon Herod, particularly as a conscience, and Herodias (remember, she held a grudge against him: Mark 6:19) in a more bitter way, yet the crowds had proceeded to follow Jesus, which was as John had predicted and intended.

Let us tease this out a little more. What would be required in our day to produce such an interesting impact upon a community of faith? The necessities appear to me to be three: firstly, someone is identified who has something worth saying; secondly, they need the independent platform which can only be given by the Church at risk to its credibility; and thirdly, the style of address and way of saying things must be sufficiently striking to produce the desired impact. This is not as strange an idea as may be first supposed. The model in the past may have been that of the itinerant evangelist, stirring the flock in one place, then moving on, but for today, engagement in a local community, forming an objective but energised source of fresh inspiration that is at the same time enriching and challenging, might just be the model for this kind of ministry – different, but using the same principles in rural and urban locations.

Built-in obsolescence is characteristic of this kind of specialised ministry, which doesn't move on until the increase has taken place. It is independent of the growth of the Church and sees the responsibility for it entirely with the working of the Holy Spirit – using the gifts of women and men of faith and commitment, but turning their words and actions to good effect. A few people of all ages modelled on John the Baptist, decreasing whilst others increase, might just be that for which the Church is crying out!

Section Two

Day 9 to Day 15
'Concerning Water'

The Water of Eternal Life – A Healing at the
Poolside – A Miracle at the Lakeside – A Storm
on the Sea

Day 9
St John's Gospel, chapter 4 verse 10: 'Jesus answered her, "If you knew the gift of God, and who it is that is saying to you, 'Give me a drink' you would have asked him, and he would have given you living water."'

This is a peculiarly challenging moment: the meeting of Jesus and the Samaritan woman at the well. 'Testing' might be better, for that is what Jesus appears to be setting up, as the encounter continues from one searching question to another penetrating observation. The discomfort of the woman is a product of the lifestyle she has embraced, and her residual acceptance of her society's common standards under the law, that causes her reticence in admitting her unorthodox path of life.

What makes the really telling difference, and something it takes the woman some time to appreciate, is that Jesus is opening a legitimate new way for her. He links his comments to what they are both physically engaged with at that time – getting water. Jesus uses the idea of thirst, so clear to them both at that moment at the well, to find a chink in this woman's armour. She is well practised in maintaining her protective carapace however, and Jesus chooses to wear it down gradually.

Thinking of other meetings that Jesus had with individuals who needed help, for one reason or another, the gentle but very firm way appears to be the approach he uses. This cannot be taken as any particular pattern for us to follow, but we are able to observe how someone, with the insight to know that something is wrong, but not the knowledge to get out of the situation, may be helped by our Lord.

Let us take someone with an habitual sin, or an unfortunate habit, or on-going relationship problems, or whatever; someone who recognises that there is a problem, may even identify what it is, but can do nothing about it. Some kind of ongoing advice through mentoring, spiritual direction or the finding of a soul friend may make the difference, and break the cycle of addiction to one particular weakness. What this verse, under consideration today, seems to imply is that we should turn our eyes away from what we lack and focus them on what Christ has to offer.

This is a very spiritually fulfilling method of facing the vicious circle of actions, thoughts or words – or conceivably a combination of two or all three of them – and breaking that circle by introducing a focus on Jesus. That focus may have already been there amongst others, but at this point our Lord must be contemplated in intimacy and honesty. This will aid the breaking of any long-term concentration on number one, and everything that goes into ensuring that the pedestal, though unsteady, cannot fall. As the woman at the well found, being tested by Jesus, though difficult in itself, produced the desired effect of making an honest realignment of her life not only possible, but blessed by Christ. If we can aid another, or have the grace to be aided in our turn, we may find that life will change and we shall discover new avenues of service and discipleship in him.

Day 10
St John's Gospel, chapter 4 verse 42: 'They said to the woman, "It is no longer because of your words that we believe, for we have heard for ourselves, and we know that this is indeed the Saviour of the world".'

The Church appears to be fairly constantly in the public eye when there are controversial matters under debate, but take an ordinary Sunday in an ordinary parish across Ireland and the silence of outside observation is deafening. 'Why does the Church not speak out?' is only too often the cry of the frustrated parishioner, who sees the sidelining of the Church in the moral, and sometimes even spiritual, wranglings of our day. When we hear, 'The Church' in this context, mostly we imagine a Bishop, or some other senior figure, taking on a politician or newspaper columnist; the social media allowing for the scraps, disagreements and debates to take their often rapidly developing course.

The woman at the well was, in comparison, a very old-fashioned protagonist, giving testimony of her encounter with Jesus, who, as she said, 'told me all that I ever did' (verse 39). Moving from such personal attestation to a direct connection with the source that lay in Christ himself, was a step that the Samaritans from the City of Sychar managed to take – with devastating effect: 'It is no longer because of your words that we believe, for we have heard of ourselves, and we know that this is indeed the Saviour of the world.'

This is a process of second-hand to first-hand knowledge that works both ways. That wish that 'The Church' (someone else in other words) would 'say something' allows us to be opinionated without having to face the crossfire of debate ourselves. Now that may mean that people, frustrated that they have no voice, whilst others have one and are not using it, become more extreme in their views. But the other way works too, that an individual, far from sitting back, will open a searching debate, turning back to the scriptures and to prayer, in the striving for truth. This forum is available in all parish situations, where there is a meeting of minds and hearts, in the common endeavour to seek to know Christ better.

Eschewing both a lazy, complaining frustration and a bombastic, opinionated over-confidence, the searching Christian in a thorough engagement with others and with Jesus, modelled on the meeting of the Samaritan woman and Jesus at the well near Sychar, may bring the general, second-hand conclusions about the issues of our day, both personal and affecting all, to a life-changing focus on themselves. Within this whole, transforming experience of challenge, that brings the woman to testify to the people of the City, and subsequently leads to the generation of so much positive energy in the many who heard her, there lies the simple fact that a personal encounter cannot be transferred. It may be real enough to be believed, but not immediate enough to reorder. The new life of which Jesus speaks is indeed a reordering; a resetting of the compass that moves us from comment to action and from silence to speech.

Day 11
St John's Gospel, chapter 5 verses 12–13: 'They asked him, "Who is the man who said to you, 'Take up you pallet, and walk'?" Now the man who had been healed did not know who it was, for Jesus had withdrawn, as there was a crowd in the place.'

The searching process that we have been considering over the last two days with the Samaritan woman at the well, and the subsequent need to witness and allow people to be drawn to their own encounter, is in contrast to the meeting of Jesus with the man at the pool of Bethzatha (or Bethesda or Bethsaida). This is one of the less exciting sites of a visit to Jerusalem today. Though the location is without doubt accurate, the ground level has been very substantially raised, and the remains of a church built on the place of the pools obscures what remains of the five porticos, where the sick lay in the hope of healing. As one looks down from the observation positions above this place, and the words of this story are read, with crowds of pilgrims pressing in on the same spot, it is hard to gain a sense of the miraculous. Much more memorable for most people is going into the adjacent and ancient church of St Anne to sing – for its acoustics are amazing. Groups from all nations queuing up for their turn; hymns sung in many languages.

But, it is worth concentrating the mind for a few minutes, blocking out the crowds and the confusing and fallen stonework, the lack of water and the absence of the blind, lame and paralysed, and considering the man of thirty-eight years of illness finding healing in the words of another man, whom he did not know, and whom he lost in the crowd before he had a chance to thank.

Was this a superstition, that the water of this pool gave healing to the first who entered when its surface was disturbed? All we know is that this man had waited for thirty-eight years for healing, and none had come. Jesus, in his characteristically directive way, instructed the man to take up his pallet and walk. This formula of restoration Jesus employs more than once, indicating that there is a point in this healing beyond the actual physical cure. The man who was healed was questioned by the Jews, but their concern was regarding the Sabbath, whilst Jesus had been concerned for the individual.

Holistic care, by its very nature, arises from concentrated attention to the whole person; this takes time, patience and a will to recognise that being a carer involves more than treating the immediate problem. The way that patients in hospital are spoken to and about is now universally improved in this respect. No one is any more, 'the appendix in bed four' or 'the hip who is away to physio', but Joe Smith or whoever. Jesus often addressed the person at the level of their underlying plight; maybe it was a fault, a sin, or a mental blockage, such as wealth or even family. He could be telling in his challenge and left some people sad, unable to go his way, others were released from some bond, but no one left wounded, save those who rejected him.

Day 12 – The Second Sunday in Lent
St John's Gospel, chapter 5 verse 24: 'Truly, truly, I say to you, he who hears my word and believes him who sent me, has eternal life; he does not come into judgement, but has passed from death to life.'

The Fourth Gospel contains many valuable things from which to learn. One whole area of our concern and observation is that of relationship. From the Prologue, the beginning of chapter 1 there is insistence on the 'Word', on what comes forth from God, being the vehicle of operation. Christ's relationship to the Father, in a fellowship of love with, and empowered by, the Holy Spirit, brings independent life into being, but thereby establishes a new and unique relationship between God and Creation that is forever tied to the nature of the Trinity. This is expressed in love, and in that divine nature, but also in purpose.

As the Gospel account by St John proceeds, so this relationship of purpose, as much as that of love and fellowship, becomes a dominant feature of our Lord's actions and words. The 'signs' express it, the 'glory' is revealed by it; the creative contact between Christ and his followers is energised ultimately by the relationship between the Son and the Father. This remains both our joy and our hope, as we as frail human beings see our lives in one sense in a perpetual state of decay, but in another of constant renewal. What John witnesses, in much that we still have to experience in the chapters that lie ahead this Lent, is to a God whose presence and purpose is revealed in Christ's very life. It is in the imitation of that life that we grow nearer to an understanding of the love of the Father, and what that means to us in the scheme of existence, that extends beyond the brief span of our mortal life, to the eternal promises upon which we rest.

So we listen to Jesus, as did his disciples, and in hearing his word, our minds are drawn to consider the Father. This is a great deal more than a source of comfort, but an intensely practical way of seeking to comprehend why we are here; what purpose each of our lives may have, and a help in trying to decipher the ways of God; of the paths of life, of judgement, of the division of sheep and goats; of the place of forgetfulness in the pilgrim's progress in life and in death. In passing from the one to the other, in the fullness of the time, Jesus demonstrates that having already, spiritually, passed the other way, the crisis has already been assimilated into the process of exposing our lives to the all-seeing, but pure and loving eyes of him, in whom we can glimpse the glory of God himself.

This is a day to look deep into the further things, but we do so in the person of Jesus, the loving Son of a loving Father. That relationship is at the heart of all we cling to as children of faith; it brings us to new life, allowing us to pass from death to life.

Day 13
St John's Gospel, chapter 6 verse 5: 'Lifting up his
eyes, then, and seeing that a multitude was coming to
him, Jesus said to Philip, "How are we to buy bread,
so that these people may eat?"'

In April 2012, I went with a small group on pilgrimage, following the Exodus route from the Nile through Sinai to Jordan. The last place we stayed in was Amman. Whilst browsing in the hotel shop I was surprised to see a number of Ladybird books that they must have had in stock for years. I suppose they were kept for children of other nationalities for the chance to practise their English language in the traditional, simple, large print style of the Ladybird book so loved by children and their parents of fifty years ago.

I have no idea whether or not a picture of the feeding of the five thousand appears in a Bible story Ladybird book, but I have in my imagination just such a representation: a simple, clear illustration and just enough text to compose the story in an attractive way for children. Many of us continue with the Ladybird picture of Christianity for the whole of our lives. The pictures are formed early in life and remain forever. I recall a Ladybird book that I had on 'Lord Nelson', or perhaps it was on 'Trafalgar', anyway, what remains with me, is the picture of the wounded Nelson prostrate, but being supported on the deck whilst the battle raged on around, but there was no blood or shattered bodies. Here was the hero of Trafalgar summoning the last of his strength to put the enemy to flight.

Such can be our idealised picture of many a biblical image, etching our minds with images of quiet scenes of Galilee, our Lord gracefully standing above and over the crowds. The reality as St John presents it in this great sixth chapter of his Gospel, is of Jesus testing his disciples and sharing with the crowd. Yet within this testing there is the child's offering. This isn't a Ladybird story, but it does rely on a child's eye-view. It is a grass-roots-up experience, beginning with the question, searching through the disciples, then through the crowd, for the answer; it comes from the boy via Andrew: 'There is a lad here who has five barley loaves and two fish.' The emphasis upon the 'much grass' and the 'five thousand' produces an expansive backdrop to the miracle. The sign of the sheer generosity of God's love, almost a profligacy (but note the baskets gathering up what remained) is then contrasted by Jesus disappearing from the scene and, in a sense, fleeing into the wilderness.

This then is a far cry from a childish story, but it does present a context in which all ages and types of people are drawn to a common ground, with the common desires of humanity clear in the need for bread. We may need to go back to this 'common ground' ourselves as Lent draws us to consider what it is that stirs our grass-roots experience, that we may look once again at the important starting points of our faith; the need to share; the costs involved, and the probability that the wilderness experience is needed to be a foil for the exuberant, the expansive, and above all for the idealised and the imagined.

Day 14
St John's Gospel, chapter 6 verses 16–17: 'When
evening came, his disciples went down to the sea, got
into a boat, and started across the sea to Capernaum.
It was now dark, and Jesus had not yet come to them.'

We are now two weeks into Lent and contemplating this from the standpoint of the
disciples on the Sea of Galilee is no bad thing.
They have experienced a high point, in
witnessing the miracle of the feeding of the five
thousand (and they were involved in this and not
simply bystanders), and now they are about to
enter the storm. St John sets the scene in his
wonderful, descriptive way by a simple
statement. Yesterday we had John's scene setting
as: 'Now there was much grass in the place.',
Today it is: 'It was now dark.' These concise,
factual comments do help us to absorb the mood
of what John is trying to relate. The grass where
the crowd was gathered gave a backdrop of
spaciousness and a sense of a 'picnic in the park';
'It was now dark', is such a simple line, but takes
us in imagination to a place that is not only more
sombre, it is potentially threatening.

An undercurrent of anxiety is established
before the storm blew up; it is 'evening', it is
'dark' and 'Jesus had not yet come'. Before we
press on to establish what Jesus is doing, let us
consider how this situation may relate to that of
our own. I am thinking here primarily of the
sometimes interrelated situations of loneliness

and anticlimax; feelings of what one might describe as post-event anxiety, or even 'the morning after the night before'. It is a commonly felt experience to step from a situation where one is buoyed up and supported, into one from which these things have been removed, landing oneself with a feeling of flatness and unease, because suddenly, and it can hit quite out of the blue, the whole ambience of life has changed.

One simple example is that of the new rector who is installed into a parish, particularly his or her first incumbency, and there is a great crowd at the institution service; the preacher is upbeat, the bishop is relieved (well, that's another one filled!) and friends, family and former and new parishioners have been tearful and happy in their turn all around. Then, the next thing is that it is a new day. Even without a funeral director's phone-call at 8.00 a.m. (though that has happened more than once), just the feeling of, 'well now I am on my own' can be almost overwhelming. Of course, that rector is no more on their own than the disciples were on the lake, less so in fact, but we are contemplating feelings here – and feelings cannot be eliminated just like that. For the disciples it got worse before it got better, but the recognition that the night, the darkness, and the absence of Jesus, were real, was important in determining that their trust in him was not a product of feelings, but the reality of faith. Feelings are important, but faith is vital, if the dark night is to be met with the knowledge of the love of God, which does not fail, and the memory of the experience of miracle fresh in the hearts of the saints.

Day 15
St John's Gospel, chapter 7 verses 4–5: 'His brothers
said to him, "Leave here and go to Judea, that your
disciples may see the works you are doing. For no man
works in secret if he seeks to be known openly. If you
do these things show yourself openly to the world."'

The beginning of chapter 7 of St John's Gospel
makes the break between the Galilean ministry
of our Lord and his final journey to Jerusalem,
ultimately to Calvary. This moment is marked in
the Synoptic Gospels (those of Matthew, Mark
and Luke, that bear a closer relationship to one
another than to John) by the acknowledgement
by his disciples that he is the Christ – and by the
experience of the Transfiguration; signifying our
Lord's place in the flow of salvation history, and
granting him and the disciples a moment of
strengthening grace, before the events of that first
Passiontide and Easter unfold.

St John sees it differently. For him, as he
records what was happening to Jesus and to the
disciples, and he is amongst their number, there
is an emphasis upon the proper time. This has
been a feature of this first portion of the Fourth
Gospel in any case, from the Prologue, through
the first miracle, when Jesus remarked to his
mother that his time had not yet come, to this
point, when human advice, from his brothers,
was being offered to Jesus, but our Lord was
clearly conscious that he had to follow his
Father's will. This is a point to which we shall

return in Holy Week, but already there is significant recognition of the overshadowing and deepening of the Saviour's path, that is pressing on Jesus as that path leads onwards to the Cross.

The brothers of Jesus are in a slightly different place, though the words they express may also be taken to promote an awareness of the simple truth that the Light of the World should not, indeed cannot, be hidden. However, there is a cost; and that is the questioning, prodding consideration for this day. How, in our witness to Jesus Christ, do we manage the expectations that call on us to proclaim the Good News, with the opportunities we have to produce an effective demonstration of what the love of God, revealed in his Son, means to us? Our testimony must ring true, and needs to be openly expressed, but in a way that encourages people to listen. If we simply beat the air with our words, what advantage is that? Our Lord's brothers draw attention to 'the works you are doing' and the burden of their encouragement of Jesus is concerned with actions rather than words. Most of us have no problem with this, but there lies the thought for each of us this day: What am I called to do in what situation, at what time, in order that my joy in Christ's love for me may be spread to others? This is one of the great questions for all Christians at all times – enough for one day, maybe!

Section Three
Day 16 to Day 22
'Difficult Questions'

Thirst – Sin – Sacrifice –
Blindness – The Casting of Stones

Day 16
St John's Gospel, chapter 7 verses 37–38: 'On the last day of the feast, the great day, Jesus stood up and proclaimed, "If anyone thirst, let him come to me and drink. He who believes in me, as the scripture has said, 'Out of his heart shall flow rivers of living water'."'

This, the last day of the feast of Tabernacles (the popular harvest-related festival), was a time of great rejoicing and fulfilment, so it is not surprising that St John emphasises these aspects in the way he introduces our Lord's words, which seem to recall the mind to the woman at the well of Sychar. We are in a context of completion and satisfaction here, almost complacency, with goodwill and corporate rejoicing. Into this milieu of happiness the Christ, the anointed one, with the voice of authority, addresses the satisfied crowd with these words, 'If anyone thirst, let him come to me and drink.' This is a glorious riposte to self-satisfaction. He is not trying to establish guilt or misgiving in the hearts of his readers, he seeks just those whose thirst is for something that physical food and drink cannot relieve.

Water is such a blessing to us in Ireland, though often we moan of the many days of rain, the lack of Summer sunshine and heat, but when it is warm and sunny, there is surely no more glorious landscape in the world! This is because of all the water to keep it green. Just after St Patrick's Day 2012, my wife, Helen, and I started to lay out our new garden at the Deanery; we bought and were given all sorts of plants and then tried to keep them alive through a dry period, as well as those days that were windy and wet. We watered in the dry and breezy weeks and did battle with the slugs during the dripping-wet days of June. Most things grew, a few died and had to be replaced, but what struck us most was how many plants respond, like the rest of us, to being fed and watered. The rhubarb was fantastic, sunflowers grew to twelve feet and more and, of course, the potatoes flourished.

As a child growing up in south-east London I lived on one of the busy arterial routes which have been much widened since (our house lies under the inside lane I think!). Next door to us was an elderly woman who used to fascinate us by going out to water the garden as the clouds were gathering and it was about to rain. She held that it would do most good if the soil was prepared to receive it. It is funny how things stick in the mind from one's childhood, but maybe she was making a theological point too, without knowing it.

Day 17
St John's Gospel, chapter 8 verse 8: 'And once more he bent down and wrote with his finger on the ground.'

I think that as he bends down and writes with his finger in the dust, it is clear that Jesus is preoccupying himself in the presence of the woman in this story, partially to avoid the woman's unease in his gaze, partially to challenge the men present by way of shifting their attention. It was an effective way of fulfilling these things and our Lord does it twice according to this account in John chapter 8.

Sex in general, exploitation of women, blatant inequality, more subtle modes of manipulation involving murky overlapping questions veering from the slightly inappropriate to the downright abusive, encompassing matters such as money, race, religion, frequently complicated by the misuse of authority; issues surrounding how men and women relate to one another both in heterosexual relationships and in same-sex partnerships have been matters of heated debate and division in recent years. Perhaps these things have always been high on the agenda. That agenda forms the subject matter that appears to obsess the Church and, in rather different ways, society in general. Much of this attention and obsession is far from edifying, but the reason for it is that we cannot stand back and study objectively the effects of sexualising many things in life, because if we distance ourselves, we ignore what is at the heart of problems lying in hurt, in some cases deeply damaged individual human lives.

Abuse, exploitation, injustice, homophobia, unfaithfulness, cruelty (one could go on) are, and have been, all clustered around the misunder-standing and/or misuse of the God-given gift of sex. The social media, have (like the Church, strangely enough) been part of the problem and also part of the solution, at least when the public considers individual cases, but at a broader, and in one sense deeper level, we know that the way in which scripture is interpreted defines the debate. Scripture is both a major element of the evidence as well as providing the *modus operandi*. The uncomfortable truth is that the method is part of the message, the way we treat other people growing from the outlook that we have established. The perceived strength of the conservative position is that it enshrines a clear, black and white interpretation of scripture, the considered strength of the liberal position is that it appears compassionate and contemporary. Holding a very firm view on this and any other matter may be maintained within real dialogue with others, if (and it is an important 'if') the strongly opinionated person keeps the channel open with one vital caveat, sincerely felt: 'It is always possible that I may be wrong!'

The story before us today is a case in point. Here we witness the accusation of guilt (of the sin of adultery) and it this guilt that is laid by the men present on one woman (without consideration of the man involved). Jesus is trying to get these would-be stone-throwers to recognise what they are doing. He achieves this by way of getting each man to recognise his own sinful feelings in the matter. St John makes the point that that recognition came to the eldest first.

Jesus is not condoning sin, as he speaks to the woman at the end of this passage, neither is he accusing her of anything. He has managed to show compassion and have his listeners take up a challenge to their outlook and lifestyle at the same time.

Day 18

*St John's Gospel, chapter 8 verse 28: 'So Jesus said,
"When you have lifted up the Son of man, then you
will know that I am he, and that I do nothing of my
own authority but speak thus as the Father taught
me".'*

Chapter 8 of the Fourth Gospel has many verses
upon which to comment. A strong theme
throughout the chapter centres on the point of
recognition. If Jesus cannot be seen for what he
is, then how on earth (literally, for everything is
clear in heaven) can those who have been
blinded attempt to lead those who have yet to
see?

I was reading recently one of a series of classic
works of natural history being republished by
Little Toller Books in Dorset. They are beautifully
produced and have lovely covers. The book I was
reading was *A Shepherd's Life* by W. H. Hudson.
In it he talks of the training of sheepdogs and
(amongst much of the wisdom and folklore
surrounding this part art, part science of rearing
a particular breed of dog to fulfil a special job) he
refers us to the practice of working a new young
dog with an older trained dog to give it guidance.
The conclusion that is reached is that this lesson
can only be carried out about three to six times –
no more – or the new sheepdog will learn an
almost irretrievably wrong lesson: to look to the
older dog thereafter as the other half of the
working relationship that guides the dog in its

controlling of the sheep, rather than the shepherd. The initial example of the older dog is excellent, but unless the Shepherd is very careful it can in the long run be detrimental.

Jesus, as presented by St John in the Fourth Gospel, is shown to be concerned that the Father is seen as the source of authority, even for him, whilst we day-to-day need reminding that, important though our parish church and clergy and other leaders may be, they are only there to point us to Christ. This is essentially a matter of priority, and a constant reminder of its importance does no harm at all, in putting what we believe into perspective.

If this perspective is held and we acknowledge that even if we were to lose our parish church and even that a church of our tradition was nowhere near, we could still join with others happily in the fellowship of Christ Jesus. It clarifies our reason for being on the grass-cutting rota and church cleaning, which may primarily be a commitment to a church building that we love, but in the end satisfies a desire to offer service in a broader sense. We do these things for our Lord too, not counting the cost, but renewed in love. George Herbert said a few things on this much better than I could ever hope to do in 'Teach me, my God and King, In all things thee to see'.[5] It is too hard to pick a verse for another person, it is best to go to the text of the whole hymn and read it all.

Day 19 – The Third Sunday in Lent
St John's Gospel, chapter 9 verse 2: 'And his disciples asked him, "Rabbi, who sinned, this man or his parents, that he was born blind?"'

The link between sin and misfortune, or even more trenchantly, sin and punishment, is not one easy to sustain in the modern era, as scientific and medical knowledge increases and the mystery of being born with a particular condition may be proven to be genetic. Theologically, this has always been a matter of authentic challenge to the understanding of the nature of God – as one who creates in love and cares providentially for all his children. Yet in our Lord's day this matter of uncertainty was a perfectly legitimate question which is raised by the disciples, and, indeed, if one thinks back to the Old Testament, the scriptures indicate, more than once, that the effects of sin may well be felt in the next generation.

Today, there are uncanny and persistent states of unease in some people's minds, that are brought about by 'tempting fate' or superstition, failing to 'touch wood', or indeed, by doing something that calls into question a person's legitimacy as a Christian. This kind of value judgement, assessing whether or not an individual is worthy of divine favour, is quite counter-Christian, in the sense that it is God who judges, who are we to condemn? Yet, equally,

Christians fear hypocrisy and in this sense the opinion of others is sought and valued and needs to be known, to be thoroughly clear and openly accepted, as what it in fact is: an opinion, not a judgement.

One of the readings of this Sunday in Year C of the Revised Common Lectionary (Luke 13:1–9) asks the question another way: 'those eighteen upon whom the tower of Siloam fell and killed them, do you think that they were worse offenders than all the others who dwelt in Jerusalem?' (verse 4) Jesus answers this question first of all with the words, 'I tell you, No; but unless you repent you will all likewise perish' and then adds the parable of the barren fig tree. This direct answer by Jesus still requires some pondering – in order to get at the complete answer – his entire meaning.

First, it should be noted that he gives a simple answer of 'No' to the question of linking sin with misfortune. That is good to hear and remember. But then the parable opens up the wider issue of life's fruitfulness or otherwise; very easily the mind slips into remembrances from the Sermon on the Mount, the Parable of the Sheep and the Goats and ultimately (if one can use that word to place lessons from the scriptures on some kind of scale), the Parable of the Good Samaritan. In other words, there is no need to contemplate the downside of failing to do what Jesus expects of us, just be encouraged to positively step down the path upon which our Lord is daily leading us. The water of life is the gift that sustains us on the way.

Day 20
St John's Gospel, chapter 9 verse 25: 'He answered,
"Whether he is a sinner, I do not know; one thing I
know, that though I was blind, now I see".'

There is an old expression that refers to someone who is confused by the sheer wealth of information before them: They can't see the wood for the trees. One can hold all sorts of random bits of knowledge, but the larger picture is elusive and possibly even frightening, it just seems so unknown, so unimaginable.

As I have grown older and explored, I hope more deeply, the spiritual path; as the complexity of life in the Church generally, and in the Cathedral that I serve, seems to increase, this is not an unfamiliar feeling. The daily moments of Morning and Evening Prayer, the Psalms and the Gospel reading for each day are a vital part of the grounding of all things in Christ Jesus. However confusing issues may appear, however one feels, whether elated or dragged down by events and attitudes, recourse to the inner well of salvation is the answer – simply to look to Christ: 'Though I was blind, now I see.'

Recently I read a book called *Edgelands* by Paul Farley and Michael Symmons Roberts[4]. In it the authors expose various places where people exist on the edge of all kinds of things. Quite surprisingly, for what is not an overtly Christian book, the authors took the example of some people carrying (well, actually wheeling) a large cross through an estate in the north of England to proclaim the crucifixion. They were getting a reaction from young people and children, as one might expect. The authors, after observing this incident, then went on to tell the story of the American, Arthur Blessitt, who has been doing this for forty years and has travelled over thirty-eight thousand miles. Each night he stops and seeks a place to rest the cross. In the forty years, more than half of the churches he has requested to keep his cross overnight have refused, but he has never been rejected by a bar or nightclub.

The seeing part of our Christian witness is a thoroughly vital aspect of all that we do, as those who wish to serve Christ Jesus in the world. To try to discern what is of God and what is a fabrication may be attempting to find a false dichotomy, but to glimpse divine splendour or the guidance of Christ, or the inspiration of the Holy Spirit is the practice of the presence of God, and the source of daily renewal of our spiritual sight.

Perhaps it is that the institutional Church cannot (at times) see the wood for the trees as matters of internal concern become the focus of attention, but eventually all comes back to the touchstone of Christ; we may not know how, or why or when, but the words of this blind man express so well the overriding feeling of relief as the way ahead at last appears to be clear, and we can say, 'One thing I know, that though I was blind, now I see.'

Day 21
St John's Gospel, chapter 10 verse 7: 'So Jesus again said to them, "Truly, truly, I say to you, I am the door of the sheep".'

The sight of sheep on the hillsides and fields of Ireland is such a familiar scene that we hardly notice them, except perhaps at the lambing time, when the engaging young fill the countryside with a bleating, ungainly gambolling. For the Middle Eastern shepherd, the picture is a little different, certainly in the dry regions, as Bedouin (mostly) women and children move their flocks of mixed rather scrawny sheep and arresting long-eared goats across pasture that looks, at best, like a green shadow on an otherwise parched wilderness. The Bedouin camps have tents and enclosures such as they must have looked in our Lord's day, having mentally removed the satellite dish!

The sense of wildness that we might gain on a misty damp morning anywhere from Connemara, to Donegal, the Mournes to the Wicklow Mountains – or wherever you may be tramping in sodden boots and drenched Gore-Tex – is rather different from the merciless sun of the Judean wilderness, but nonetheless the need for sanctuary is no less apparent. The shepherd is the provider of that sanctuary in each case and the image of the door is a welcome and meaningful description of the standard sign of escape.

Of course, doors may allow people to emerge to the unknown; may be taken as leading from safety to the risks of an unprotected adventure, but in the case before us today, Jesus, as the door of the sheep, is surely the gate to salvation, the way of the pilgrim, the open space for the lost and oppressed. This door of the sheep is the way into safety; it is the path to sanctuary.

Jesus himself told us that he is the 'way' as well as the 'truth' and the 'life'. This entrance to the sheepfold, that can be imagined in the mind's eye, helps the searching Christian to contemplate the combination of reassurance and welcome that is portrayed in Christ, drawing all people to himself, as everyone is inclined to stray and lose sight of the way. In Lent, there is the time, which can be given to this searching and contemplation; it is comforting too, for a new vision of just how the service of Christ, in the world, may be harnessed to a closer fellowship within the body – within his flock.

Glancing across the open expanses of open pasture land in Ireland brings so many of the old ways to mind: St Patrick as a slave, kept as a shepherd boy, praying day and night in all weathers, yet maintaining his responsibility for those sheep under his care. These are familiar, almost hackneyed illustrations of Christian concern, but nonetheless they do not lose their power, in the minds of those whose lives seek the fulfilment of the pilgrim's way.

Day 22
St John's Gospel, chapter 10 verse 22: 'It was the feast of the Dedication at Jerusalem; it was winter, and Jesus was walking in the temple, in the portico of Solomon.'

I love to read these little additions in the text, that could be done without, but add a little something extra, such as the 'it was winter' in this verse. In chapter 6 when Jesus came to the disciples walking on the water, the comment was: 'It was now dark' (verse 17); in Mark 8:14, 'and they had only one loaf with them in the boat.' All of these and other similar asides serve to remind us of the immediacy of what was happening. The Evangelists may have written each of their accounts of the Gospel story many years after the events that they record, but the freshness is readily felt – 'as though it were yesterday', as we might say over something special we remember. Some could tell you, a long time after a noteworthy occasion in their lives, what they were wearing on that day, or what flavour of ice cream they bought, or who they met or some such anecdote.

Some years ago on a holiday in the west of Ireland we stopped for a night in Easkey and went for a walk. We crossed the river on stepping stones and I lost a shoe, which began to float on down the current. Needless to say that day was remembered for that incident – the night for something rather different. There were high winds and the caravan nearly took off (the children, as they were then, slept peacefully through it all). Everyone has their memories from special occasions, holidays and anniversaries, but remembering that dress, or the weather, or the car breaking down, all help to mark the moment in the mind.

The Feast of Dedication, some three months after the Feast of Tabernacles was, like the earlier harvest festival, a happy and nostalgic time. It linked them directly to the Temple, the heart of their worship and their faith. Celebration is part of what our lives are about, part of what it means to be human, and we should take time and make an effort to mark celebrations in the way that is appropriate and meaningful. For some, this means spending lots of money, for others the modest doing of something ordinary in a special way is enough, and can cost nothing but the time and energy involved.

Somehow, and it is hard to explain, I find this introduction (to a very challenging and direct encounter between an insistent and questioning group of people and Jesus (verses 24–39)) to be an oddly comforting and calming description. This is an occasion of people coming together; the season is observed, the normality of a walk in a holy place is experienced and the scene for something wonderful to happen is established. That wonderful thing was concentrated around the confrontation shown forth in the words of the opposition: 'It is not for a good work that we stone you but for blasphemy; because you, being a man, make yourself God.' The scene is being set for all that is about to happen.

Section Four

Day 23 to Day 29

'Service and Sacrifice'

Mary and Martha – Priests and Scribes – Light
and Darkness – Water and Towel

Day 23
St John's Gospel, chapter 11 verse 5: 'Now Jesus loved Martha and her sister and Lazarus.'

This comment by St John amplifying the relationship between Jesus and this family of Bethany could be taken as an aside, such as those considered yesterday. In one sense it is, but more crucially it says something about what Christ meant to these people and what they meant to him, that goes well beyond the 'and it was dark' or 'we had one loaf of bread' type of comment. Here we are given a little window onto a special relationship; John had one such with Jesus; Mary Magdalene clearly established something similar, and, whether or not we identify this Mary with her, there is a revelation in these words that we could benefit from pondering.

'Now Jesus loved Martha and her sister and Lazarus.' 'Love' is a word that preachers are careful in handling. We usually point out that in Greek there are different words to describe its different aspects. For that between friends, love, *phileos*, is seen as a platonic, self-giving and self-effacing expression of an inner bond that is permanent. John appears to be emphasising the love of Jesus for his friends at this point, before what may be construed as an act of callousness in not immediately going to Bethany to heal Lazarus, but rather remaining some time where he was first.

We are caught up in double meanings in this chapter too, which complicates the matter further. Jesus speaks of 'this illness [that] is not unto death' (verse 4), and later, 'I go to awake him out of sleep' (verse 11). Jesus refers to mortal life and divine life in the same breath, interchanging human death with sleep and the certainty of healing with the disclosure of the glory of God.

What we make of it at this point of Lent is to pause in our proceedings (as in a way Bethany is that – a symbolic and actual resting place for Jesus and his disciples) away from the threat, immediate or otherwise, of being seen and heard in the city, just across the Mount of Olives from where they stayed. We are about at the halfway point in Lent, and, if you are still with me in my ramblings, perhaps you might like to take stock around this issue of 'love' and its implications for personal relationships.

'Love' has more than one shade of meaning, as has 'life', but together they make what we strive for, full of purpose, and link us with those whose pilgrim path is shared with our own. This may be a husband or wife, a parent or child, a friend or acquaintance at work, or Church, or involved with you in the same leisure activity. What does your 'love' for that person amount to, as you think of their 'life', in both the connotations that Jesus employs? Is it an aside that could float by, or a deepening relationship of hope and trust, such that draws you to a common purpose in Christ and under the Father's infinite care? It's worth pondering, isn't it?

Day 24

St John's Gospel, chapter 11 verses 49–50: 'Caiaphas, who was high priest that year, said to them, "you know nothing at all: you do not understand that it is expedient for you that one man should die for the people, and that the whole nation should not perish".'

No one likes to be told, even as one in a group that is so addressed, that they 'know nothing at all'. We are especially sensitive to such a negative assertion if we are talking to children or young people. But here it seems to be acceptable, because the High Priest is described as 'not say[ing] this on his own accord, but being high priest that year he prophesied'. This could be thought of as a rather poignant and ironic note, for Caiaphas, is saying that there is an answer to the question that was being posed by his fellow chief priests, Pharisees and council members. The question was 'What are we to do?' in response to the signs and miracles that Jesus was performing. It is ironic because the prophesy of the High Priest purported to save the nation through the death of Jesus, whilst what was saved was the whole world, not just the interests of the few.

There is much to be thought about around this central concern for the Christian Church in the coming weeks, as Passiontide and Holy Week approach, but for today, let us think a little of motivation and its effects. Ambition is decidedly frowned upon in the Church; in fact for an ordained person to be described as 'ambitious' is to slight that individual with the faintest of praise at getting places, but with the much stronger stain of disapproval for self-seeking success; yet ambition is one of the great motivating forces in human nature. Without ambitious people many of the great achievements of society would not occur. Ambition rightly directed may lead to good things occurring, though the sight of the bodies strewn on the ground whilst getting there hardly reflects how Christians should be approaching their endeavours in ministry and mission.

What is it that motivates you in life? Do you achieve things almost in spite of yourself or do you have a focused way of getting things done? Is a degree of ambition something that the Church should consistently deplore or do we require it of at least some of our clergy to keep the edge of focus in the senior leadership roles?

I believe that the Church should tackle this by reducing the honours of high position, and increasing the sense of challenge and privilege in being allowed to fulfil them. Jesus, after all, did place very considerable challenges in the way of his disciples, and did not deny that those who held responsible positions would be tested, but he equally demonstrated that the path of life was one of denial and cross-carrying. Many of the great and important changes that have happened in the world, that bring leaders to the forefront of public recognition, are brought about by ordinary men and women standing fearlessly in front of tanks and being taken from their homes and families and incarcerated for years for bravely standing for what is right. Such motivation in the cause of the Kingdom of God is in keeping with Christian discipleship.

Day 25

St John's Gospel, chapter 12, verse 3: 'Mary took a pound of costly ointment of pure nard and anointed the feet of Jesus and wiped his feet with her hair; and the house was filled with the fragrance of the ointment.'

On one occasion when I was with a group on pilgrimage to the Holy Land, on visiting a church in Cana, where Jesus turned the water into wine, there was to be a special celebration later that day. I can't remember exactly what it was; I think that the relics of a saint were being brought to the church, but I am not sure. Anyhow, the point that I want to make is this: that the celebration was being marked by the whole sanctuary of the church being filled – and I mean literally *filled* with flowers. Not the usual two vases placed on pedestals or shelves either side of the altar, but pots and troughs, stands and great and small containers of cut blooms. A brown-habited friar snipped and adjusted, moving with devotional care; quietly and in an absorbed manner he lovingly tended and arranged.

Perfume and flowers are such intrinsically important gifts, redolent of loving attention to the object of our desire, that they can become almost shockingly revealing of our state of emotional engagement. Perhaps I put this too strongly. For some a silk imitation or, worse still, a dusty plastic attempt at colour is no different to rapidly fading natural blossom, but to gather the correct impression of Mary of Bethany it is essential to appreciate that something wonderful; an act of pure devotion is occurring here.

That this incident shocked and was remembered is hardly surprising: a woman anointing the feet of Jesus, and wiping them with her hair, is a scene filled with a mysterious connotation of inner understanding between two people that places the observer just as that – an observer. We are inclined to rationalise the moments when we see the surface action, but cannot fully discern the hidden effect. The Samaritan woman at the well tried this ploy, to absorb what Jesus was trying to show her. Judas attempts to bring this incident, at the beginning of John chapter 12, to some acceptable level of normality by complaining about the waste of ointment. But all this misses the point, doesn't it? The point is that in Mary we have the devoted soul expressing her love for Jesus, and her joy too, in his presence, in a way that others could only gape at.

I think of that young friar at Cana, soft-footed, handling the delicate petals, leaves and stems with just the devoted tenderness with which Mary used her hair, to spread the ointment and remove its excess from the feet of Jesus. For days she would have carried that scent with her, as in sorrow the days were coming when she would carry the crucifixion of our Lord within her; both expressions of love; both holding the imprint of the divine life on the human soul.

Day 26 – The Fourth Sunday in Lent – Mothering
Sunday
St John's Gospel, chapter 12, verse 35: 'Jesus said to
them, "The light is with you for a little longer. Walk
while you have the light, lest the darkness overtake
you; he who walks in the darkness does not know
where he goes".'

One of the appointed Gospel readings for Mothering Sunday is also from St John (chapter 19, verses 25–27) and considers one of the darkest possible moments for any mother, as Mary beholds the crucifixion of her son and is given the care of the beloved disciple as he is of she. This most emotive and heart-wrenching of all the words of our Lord from the Cross, settles the place of human relationships within the greater darkness and light of eternal understanding.

For most of us, the fear of darkness is real and caught up with loneliness and blindness. Shortly after my wife and I were married we rented a cottage on the Isle of Man from a lovely elderly lady from 'Queen's County'. She had left Ireland in the 1930s and settled in the middle of the Irish Sea in the little island that is my wife's native land. Miss Hankinson was of that fearless tradition of maiden octogenarians (of which I have known quite a few) that seem to be undeterred from the usual things that feed most people's anxieties. To walk in darkness from her cottage down a twisting lane to the beach would be a soft stroll in the quiet of a still night, protected by the presence of God, rather than a frightening experience of gloomy, shadow-cast moonlight, weird shapes leaping into sight from hedges, to scare the prickly and vivid imagination.

'The light is with you a little longer' is such a comforting thought for the glass half-full people of this world – and a little scary for the glass half-empty ones! Driving along the roads of Ulster, though less so than a few years ago, there are still plenty of warning signs placed by the local residents to remind us to think: 'Where will you spend eternity?' Or simply, 'Eternity where?' Remember 'The wages of sin are death.' Or, with a more positive message, 'Jesus saves.'

I have two problems with this: first, that I don't believe Jesus ever intended us to be scared into the Kingdom of Heaven; and second, and more pointedly, surely the mission to which we are committed is one focussed on what we are giving, rather than on what we are hoping to receive. By walking in the light we are clearly on the opposite tack to those who are simply concerned about sailing away from what frightens them, whether that is eternal punishment or more understandably 'darkness'. That does not necessarily lead into the light. Rather let us look to the light that we have and walk in it; it is with us a little longer. As Mary looked up at the Cross and saw her son; as John took his new responsibility to heart and as we look onwards to Holy Week, let us hold the light of Christ in our hearts for one another and not succumb to fear, but walk our path with courage and hope.

Day 27
St John's Gospel, chapter 13, verse 5: 'Then he poured water into a basin, and began to wash the disciples' feet, and to wipe them with the towel with which he was girded.'

In the days when it was common to have one's feet washed on arriving in someone's house, the act of washing another person's feet was seen to be the work of a servant. Today, in twenty-first century Ireland, our greeting of another is more likely to be a kiss and a hug, or the shake of a hand whilst receiving a coat and perhaps a small gift. Washing dusty, sandal-bound, but otherwise, bare, feet is not common this side of the Middle East or North Africa. Where we liturgically incorporate our Lord's act of humility is generally on Maundy Thursday, when the Last Supper is celebrated. To source twelve parishioners happy to enact this moment of the meal, asks I believe, in our day, as much of them as it does of the priest presiding – more perhaps.

Humility is a subject like poverty that is only virtuous when it is undertaken willingly; if imposed or otherwise has to be lived with, those involved are in a quite different place. That said, I heard John Bell (of Iona) on the radio talking about the Beatitudes on a Sunday service last July. He expressed the thought that it was only when he considered the opposite of the conditions of blessedness that he understood why the poor in spirit, the meek, and those who mourn, are seen to be granted happiness. Of course, much of the Sermon on the Mount needs to be taken in this spirit.

A few days of this book were written during the course of the Olympic Games, which, at least in the UK, had wall-to-wall coverage, and tomorrow I will reflect a little further on them, but in terms of the reactions of people, we experienced the whole spectrum of response to success and failure and even to what those things represent. The watching public are warmed by the happy but gracious victor and the tearful, but gallant loser; what it longs for is to witness hard work and commitment – success rewarded – and, if the truth be told, a degree of national glory. The acknowledgement that someone else is better than us (or – often more to the point – our son or daughter, wife, husband, grandchild, etc.) is something that is part of our maturing as a human being and most particularly as a Christian disciple.

If this reflection was to be 5,000 rather than 500 words, I would be tempted to start surrounding this discussion with all sorts of caveats, such as how important it is to be honest with oneself, what turning the eyes to other things does for us spiritually, etc. But in the end humility doesn't need caveats. None of us have the humility of Christ, all of us suffer from the pride of Adam who knew better than God, or thought he did. Neither should we beat ourselves with the stick of our conscience. Christ's act at the

Last Supper in washing the disciples' feet was an act of love. Acts of love are what he asks of us. We shall fail, but occasionally we shall also succeed, and come to realise that from time to time we are learning from the coach, from Jesus, not to make us capable of winning a gold medal, but for another faltering step in the right direction.

Day 28
St John's Gospel, chapter 13, verse 35: 'By this all men will know that you are my disciples, if you have love for one another.'

I was on holiday for most of the extent of the London 2012 Olympic Games and so watched a great deal more of the events than I was likely to have done had I been at home in Belfast. We were on the Isle of Man visiting family and the old haunts of my wife from childhood. It was all slightly surreal, because at the same time I was watching some of the places that for me held memories from long ago. I was born and brought up in Blackheath and the Heath and Greenwich Park (scene of the horse riding) were my local play areas. The Olympic Village and Stadium are not a hundred miles from where I spent most of my school days and even Weymouth held the distant vision of a very happy week on a biology field trip – topped by winning a can of Newcastle Brown by being able to identify the golden saxifrage without the aid of a pictorial guide; one of my very few claims to success.

It is funny how things will stick in the memory, but our outlook is certainly coloured by what we cling to, what we love and dwell on, what we choose to spend our time doing, and we can surprise ourselves by the strength of affection for things we thought were maybe long gone. However, the directing of our attention by the media, social or professional, is a cause for even greater wariness. There was an especially obvious example of this, during the second week of the Olympic Games, as Ireland sought its first medal and Team GB was verging on the raucous in celebrating success. As the news switched from London to Damascus, from Eton Dorney to West Africa, from the Serpentine to Afghanistan, I was struck again and again by the imbalance of our news diet.

When Jesus says, 'By this all men will know that you are my disciples, if you have love for one another,' he does so without dictating how that love should be expressed. He does give us plenty of teaching on the subject, from his parables to his miracles, from his sermons and ultimately from the example of his own life and death, but it is for us to translate this teaching into a relevant approach to Christian discipleship in our day. Are our hearts touched more by the needs of others or by our need to express love for another? Somewhere in there, in that question, lies the answer to the ongoing source of our desire to live the Christian life, not as an individual primarily, but as one in community; in a fellowship of believers.

As the demands of our past and present impinge upon how we see our need to express our love for others, both today and tomorrow, holding the focus on 'the moment', that which is passing and can never be repeated is crucial. Jesus lived 'the moment' to the full and the Gospels express this for us; he drew on the past, and planned for the future ministry of the Church, but he loved others that day, that hour, that moment for them, as an expression of his inner desire placed there by the Father, and which grew through prayer to be what could and did take him to the Cross. We need no greater incentive or example.

Day 29
St John's Gospel, chapter 14, verse 8: 'Philip said to him, "Lord, show us the Father, and we shall be satisfied".'

The need to 'see' is a natural enough impulse for human beings. 1000 places to visit before you die has been expanded sufficiently to ensure that we will also see, hear, taste and touch – and probably smell as well – a huge number of extraordinary sensory experiences before we are all very much older. This is a way of dealing with the Western World's obsession with trying to grasp the meaning of what a fulfilling life consists. Even the *Irish Times* (such a comforting bastion of good sense) succumbed with its *A History of Ireland in 100 Objects*. But does what we 'see' really give us the understanding that we need?

For Philip to 'see' was paramount. It was to his mind what would bring satisfaction, peace of mind if you like, to him and to his fellow disciples. The sight of the Father, he must imagine, as being such that his tendency to distraction, doubt and worry would be instantly removed. Jesus, knowing this to be literally, physically impossible in any case, was drawn into further explanation as to what 'seeing the Father' amounted to in reality. The whole argument we may understand in a critical way, when viewing Philip's request from the vantage point of many years of Christian reflection. However, before we get too sure of ourselves, let *turned towards us*

? us consider the obverse position to that taken for this request, namely the clear understanding that the sight of Jesus is the sight of the Father.

We can appreciate that Jesus reflects the Father's love, compassion and humility, yet perhaps at the same time, also envisage a wrathful God at the heart of Christian experience; though this is difficult to maintain on the evidence of the Gospels. As we approach the Passion of our Lord in the coming two weeks, there is little room for imagining that he is doing anything other than fulfilling the Father's desire, as well as his will for him. They are one, as Jesus emphasises again and again in this chapter; the Father and the Son in unity of purpose and love. For me, the modern hymn[6] that has the line, 'The Father turns his face away' at the crucifixion, an expression of the theological understanding of the nature of the rending of the relationship within the Trinity, raises a profound question, which is relevant to this point of seeing Jesus as being the same as seeing the Father.

So where do we 'see' the Father if not in Jesus? If, on the Cross, we no longer see the Father in the Son, but the Son alone; wrenched from the Father's eyes (as well as his love?) by the will of the Father himself, where does this leave our understanding of the Holy Spirit's presence in our lives and in our spiritual sight?

Christ's words to Philip are the reassurance that comes from understanding that 'seeing' is not 'believing' or even understanding; fulfilment, or 'satisfaction', as Philip puts it, is due to an inner conversion that relies not on the senses, but rather on the heart and soul being touched by the love of God in Christ and thereby draws us into that unity which is found at Calvary.

Section Five

Day 30 to Day 32

'The Last Supper'

Peace – Hope – Joy – Prayer –
Sight – Sacrament – Unity

Day 30
St John's Gospel, chapter 14, verse 27: 'Peace I leave
with you; my peace I give to you; not as the world
gives do I give to you. Let not your hearts be troubled,
neither let them be afraid.'

The peace of Christ, the peace of God, which
passes our understanding – we share a sign of
this peace and pray for its enduing in every
celebration of the Eucharist. How many times, I
wonder have I read this verse from John
chapter 14, tagged on to the first 6 or 11 verses at
a funeral? There are words from this text that
leap out at one: the 'world', 'be troubled', 'be
afraid'. Each is introduced with a negative. A
negative perception met with a negative
intention. The force that this gives to the passage
is considerable. This peace is not just to be seen
as an antidote to turmoil, it is of a different order
to the normal flow of human existence. The
'world' gives peace too, but not as Christ gives it.
Peace in the world is seen as the answer to
conflict; the striving to bring people together in
harmony, but the peace of God is of the heart;
outwardly expressed maybe in a lightness of
being, and joy in action and word, but within is
stability; a core designed in the perfect
sufficiency of love.

This peace is needed for the Christian to
operate in some kind of close relationship to
others, as well as sharing in the desire and intent
of Christ as Lord and brother. As Jesus spoke

these words to his disciples, surely the reassurance was being built up that they were not alone, and the fundamental reasoning behind the Holy Spirit's presence (once Jesus physically left them) was starting to seep into their consciousness. At least this was the hope and prayer of our Lord himself – as it remains to our day.

If we are presently envisaging that the peace that this world gives is the same as that of God himself, and that trouble and fear are the natural outcome of living a human life, then the step to accepting the peace of Christ in our hearts is one that we need to seek to take. There is much that lies ahead in the Passion of Christ that we enter in the coming days, which will bring us to the point of darkness, as we contemplate the suffering and desolation of our Lord on the Cross. Let us at this moment try to remember what the disciples forgot, namely the promise of the peace of Christ being literally 'left' with us. I really love that expression which holds the picture to me of a carefully given parting gift; a treasure that may have no monetary worth, but is a gift of the heart from one person to another in love. It is held out to us week by week, day by day, lest we forget and run, like the disciples, to our own thoughts and troubles and fears, or even from them, to some form of temporary escape.

Day 31
St John's Gospel, chapter 15, verse 8: 'By this my Father is glorified, that you bear much fruit, and so prove to be my disciples.'

It is said that a clergyman of the Church of Ireland on some occasion approached his Bishop with the words, 'Bishop, I am not happy in my parish.' To which the Bishop replied, 'You are not here to be happy, you are here to work!' I will leave you to guess the Bishop, but I don't think that it is a remark that we are likely to hear these days. Today we would take a compassionate view that holds the premise that if you are fulfilled and enjoy what you are doing, then the work will just happen naturally.

The right balance between what is expected of us, and what we are prepared to give in life is a delicate one and over the past few financially stringent years the contrast between industry and profligacy has been underlined again and again. The Christian moralist can be seen as a very stick-in-the-mud, dour, kill-joy, if he or she suggests that the get-rich-quick; if-you-can-get-away-with-it-good-on-you, sailing-close-to-the-wind-financially, so-long-as-no-one-knows-it-doesn't-matter attitude to grey areas of day-to-day living is wrong. Flexibility is the name of the game. Into this mishmash of human nature we throw the controlling fences of health and safety, protocols, guidelines and all the bits of paper that cushion us from ourselves; from our tendency to go our own way and do our own thing.

Several times in the Gospels those who came to Jesus sought the same hedging round of their duty to God and each other: 'And who is my neighbour?' 'What must I do to gain eternal life?' etc. Jesus gives us a very different impulse for work towards bearing fruit. He suggests to the disciples that the Father is glorified and they are proved to be disciples if they bear fruit. No pressure then! But that is the point isn't it? There is pressure if the terms and conditions of our discipleship are laid out like a contract of employment, but the release of being expected merely (I use the word advisedly) to bear fruit is one of the joys of being a disciple of Jesus. We are talking here of something that lifts us from the grind of what is demanded, to the excitement and sheer wanton desire to bring glory to God, whose very presence in our lives, our hearts and our work for the Kingdom, is beyond measure.

Why do people continue to strive for the treasure that rots and rusts? Why do we need to face the rigours of suffering and the threat of death before we come to our senses? Because we are caught in the pattern of the world, which cannot understand that love is the heart of all things; and that God is love. We shall shed much of our anxiety if we truly desire what Christ alone holds out for our good, for our acceptance, and in return our joy alone will bring us to bear fruit for his glory.

Day 32
St John's Gospel, chapter 15, verse 11: 'These things I have spoken to you, that my joy may be in you, and that your joy may be full.'

A Saturday for many people is the beginning of the weekend and a day off work. For the retired, the self-employed and those who work shifts in shops and public service, it may well be the same as any other day. For years, when our children were at school, I took Saturday as my day off – not a good idea really, because I always spent some time on my sermon too, reading through and making minor changes (nearly always adding stuff that it could probably have done without!). Anyway, time off, to relax, play or watch sport, garden and generally socialise or spend time with family, friends or at a hobby is what we may see as the happiest time of the week. There is something good and healthy and life-giving about this and retirement strikes me from afar (well not so far as it was!) as having a lot of these elements about it. But this is not what Jesus is getting at with regard to 'Joy'.

Joy is a gift. It is the essence of what it means to share love with one another. It is the participation in the life of Christ. It does something to us within that lifts us to a place of fulfilment that is not dependent on human success or satisfaction. We sacrifice joy when the heart is not tuned to the things of God. We find joy when we know within ourselves that the path that we take, however hard, however painful, is where Christ wants us to be. This is difficult for those whose fluctuating commitment to Jesus and to the Church is exactly that; wavering, half-hearted, occasional. That goes for most of us …

Lent, if we are to take a critical look at ourselves during it, is not a time for forty-odd days of the angst of self-criticism. It is an opportunity, having accepted that we are not all that we should be, to spend some time in deepening a commitment to prayer and action, that Christ's joy may be in us and that our joy may be full. We are set on a process of realignment that may mean finding this joy through self-giving of our time and talents in the service of God; perhaps giving money to further the mission of the Church either here or overseas; maybe there are other things to which our minds will turn, that open windows on to a fresh understanding of something to do with our faith.

Whatever outcome our Lenten discipline may have, there is surely the chance to find within us a little more space that Christ can occupy and within our lives an opportunity to show a love and joy in believing that brings light and hope to others. This may well lead us to discover the true depth of joy that lies within us; a joy that Christ wills for us to make complete.

Section Six

Day 33 to Day 39

'Passiontide'

Day 33 – The Fifth Sunday in Lent – Passion Sunday
St John's Gospel, chapter 16, verse 16: 'A little while,
and you will see me no more; and again a little while,
and you will see me.'

This Sunday begins Passiontide. It is still Lent, but the feel of the Penitential Season takes upon it the closer realisation that Holy Week and the Crucifixion of Jesus are imminent. Gone are the stones of the wilderness. Now the focus is entirely on Jerusalem, Bethany, where Mary and Martha and Lazarus provide a home-from-home for Jesus and his disciples, and upon the significance of the Passover.

Jesus is indicating that things are about to change for him and for his nearest friends and disciples. Those about him recognise the threat to Jesus, and to them all by being in Jerusalem and under critical scrutiny whenever they are in public. Jesus has drawn attention to himself and next Sunday, especially, we shall note this as he makes his symbolic entry on a donkey to the shout of 'Hosanna'. But later that week, at the Last Supper, Jesus gives instruction to the disciples that would not be understood by them then, but later they would come to see what he was saying to them. Amongst these things is the slightly confusing and almost secretive saying: 'A little while, and you will see me no more; and again a little while, and you will see me.'

It is really hard to be prepared for something we are dreading is going to happen, that we have recognised as being a distinct possibility, when that possibility becomes a probability, maybe a certainty. While we have the hope that what we fear may not happen, we can fool ourselves into thinking that it definitely won't. I know that our particular view may be coloured by whether we are a glass-half-full person, or a glass-half-empty person. I suppose we are particularly adept at dealing with this when it is a matter of our health, some swinging the way of living in denial, others, just the opposite, becoming hypochondriacs.

Spiritually, we may suffer the same crisis of conscience; either feeling undermined in our faith to such an extent that we are cutting ourselves adrift from the scriptures, or so certain that we cannot allow those who present legitimate doubts to speak to us at all – at least seriously and meaningfully.

So, our attitude on this Sunday needs to find the right pitch in tracing the ways of our Lord to the Cross. Within that path we shall encompass many places from Olivet to Calvary, but let us try to do so with an openness of heart and mind that seeks to learn from a loss of sight and a seeking to regain it. Four days ago we thought about seeing in a rather different way, as we sought the face of God in the face of Jesus; now we seek to see where we may only experience the darkness of the opposition, arrest, trial and crucifixion of Jesus. It is a dark path, but it has its own way of showing us more than we may know, and definitely more than we expect.

Day 34
St John's Gospel, chapter 16, verse 33: 'In the world you have tribulation; but be of good cheer, I have overcome the world.'

We need look no distance at all to see people suffering from persecution and tribulation of all kinds. Millions of Christians are still persecuted in the world today, a thing that is easy to forget in our take-it-or-leave-it attitude to Christianity in Britain and Ireland. How would we fare if we really had to stand up and be counted?

This verse does take the argument a step further though, as Jesus explores in the disciples' minds the ultimate meeting of good and evil, not only in this time, but universally. We need to broaden our understanding of tribulation, to encompass the cosmic enterprise in which Jesus is engaged, and the 'World' as representative of the crisis of the fallen 'Creation'. It is too small a thing to imagine this claim, and striking comment by Jesus, as simply a reference to their directly experienced few days in Jerusalem, concentrated and threatening though they may be.

The Celtic Saints were adept at placing the context of their prayer and reflection in this wider sphere of physical and spiritual understanding. They somehow knew that their closeness to the Divine was reflected in their closeness to the whole created order. That may be through the elements of daily contact with water, land and air, with animals, plants and the greater and lesser lights in the heavens, but within all human experience they knew the active presence of Christ. His sense of overcoming was paralleled in the way that their lives conformed to a realism, that was glimpsed through the inner eye of a faith, that expected to see the extraordinary in the ordinary and the Godly in the banal.

Life was tough in the Celtic settlements of the early Christians in these islands, and Ireland was a peculiarly important cradle for the shifting, spirit-filled devotion of the saints, who occupied many remote communities and hermit cells. I am very familiar with a number of these ancient hermitages or keills on the Isle of Man. There is one at Lag-ny-Killey on the western side of the glowering mass of Cronk-na-Airey-Laa. It is reached along a path, no wider than a sheep track, through bracken and rough grass. The level area, marked by the stones of a small ruined chapel, and those of an even tinier dwelling, is one of the places that, with a little imagination, reflects the language of an overcoming Christ. The spaciousness around the sparseness shows, without words or gesture, that the hermit, who spent his life at this spot, knew the rigours of physical striving – with the open mind of the solitary. This was no escape from ultimate tribulation, but a place to learn that Christ has overcome the world. We too can find that truth, not just at the edges of perception in a place of barrenness, but in the quiet inner transformation of a heart, even in the midst of a busy city, that is turned to the contemplation of Christ's sacrifice upon the Cross.

Day 35
St John's Gospel, chapter 17, verse 11: 'Holy Father, keep them in thy name, which thou hast given me, that they may be one, even as we are one.'

The chapter 17 of Saint John's Gospel consists of what has become known as Christ's *High Priestly Prayer*. He is interceding for his disciples in it, praying for them and their relationship with the world around them, for their unity and for their security. To know that at the source of all our strivings there is Jesus, without whom we can do nothing. We pray for his working within us; for the inspiration of the Holy Spirit; for direction, strength and at times, simply the right words to say in a difficult situation.

The Church (and I suppose I am thinking of it in its institutional, parochial, local representation here) can get itself caught in the position of only appearing to offer a sanctuary for those who want to separate themselves from the world, be it for an hour on a Sunday, or for a more permanent escape, creating a world within a world of private devotion. There is an element of this about the form and intent of the Church that it does, in both its institutionalised structure and its inner spiritual life, provide just the kind of sanctuary that Jesus seems to prepare his disciples for in the extensive prayer for them in John 17. Jesus describes his nearest followers as 'in the world' but not 'of the world'.

Parish churches can come to be this supporting spiritual, social and practical centre of a community very effectively, and have been so for centuries. The problem that many are finding now though is that, having embraced this model of Church, it is hard to change the mindset, to see that this place of sanctuary is effectively only recognised, and hence (in reality) open, to a tiny proportion of the population and that the real mission of the Church has all but dried up. This may not be the case in rural areas of Ireland, but in the towns and cities the Church has long come to realise that it needs to be 'out there' as a visible presence in the community. The Church has been told for long enough that it exists for those beyond its fellowship, but the sense of its role of sanctuary is still strong – nor do we want to lose it – but surely not at the expense of its mission.

Jesus does say to the Father in this prayer, 'As thou didst send me into the world, so I have sent them into the world.' By this he indicates how his disciples must seek to be what they still are: a community within a community; a body of his followers that will make their presence felt as they challenge and serve, fulfil his (i.e. Christ's) mission as healer and reconciler in the world around them.

But there is an intimacy revealed in this prayer, that not only shows the love and understanding between the Father and the Son, it renews the sense of sharing that should always be part of the disciple's place within the fellowship of the Church and in direct relationship with our Lord.

Day 36
St John's Gospel, chapter 17, verse 20: 'I do not pray for these only, but also for those who believe in me through their word.'

The prayer that we began yesterday, the *High Priestly Prayer*, with which Jesus implored his Father, contains a great deal concerning the immediate circle of his disciples. This is at the Last Supper. Our Lord is about to be arrested and tried, condemned and crucified, but Jesus is already beyond this in his thought and prayer for others. He will have his own moment with the Father in an agony of supplication in the Garden of Gethsemane, but here in the Upper Room, the focus is on the mission; on the Gospel message being proclaimed and lived in a post-resurrection world.

The Apostles are not ready, nothing like it, but they will be entrusted with the responsibility anyway – and they will have the presence and power of the Holy Spirit to aid them in all that they undertake. So it is that Jesus is not only praying for them, but is also praying for those who will receive the Word of God from their lips.

Most clergy reach the point at some time that they are about to knock on the door of someone in trouble, or climb into the pulpit with a difficult sermon to preach, or chair a meeting that they fear may be fraught with dissension and they literally or metaphorically get down on their knees with the prayer, 'I cannot do this! I can only face it in your strength.' Daily we pray in a similar fashion for the guidance and inspiration of the Holy Spirit, but there are times in all of our lives when it strikes home with a particular, inner crisis of confidence. Afterwards, there is almost always a sense of both release and a realisation that we coped much better than we expected. Take that as coincidence if you like, but for me it demonstrates the power of prayer, and the need to use such heartfelt pleas to the Father not just at the moment of crisis.

Jesus, in verse 20, raises the point for us today that there is a crucial relationship within the whole ministry of the Church that needs careful attention, in order that people may come to believe. That relationship is between those who are of the fellowship of the Church and those who are beyond it. Now this may be obvious; something to which we turn our thoughts and prayers all of the time, but sometimes the obvious is the last thing we actually notice. Individual churches can be challenged beyond their willingness to change by an influx of new believers, and adaptability is something that we may or may not have at any age!

The matter for us to think about today is, 'Do I have the desire, as Jesus had, to see beyond what the Church I attend *is*, to what it may *become*?' 'Do I, in fact, pray for those beyond the worshipping community of which I am a part with the intention that the Kingdom may increase and that I will continue to be challenged by the inspiring and transforming power and guidance of the Holy Spirit?'

Day 37
St John's Gospel, chapter 18, verse 2: 'Now Judas, who betrayed him, also knew the place; for Jesus often met there with his disciples.'

The character of Judas is one that arouses sympathy as well as condemnation. He is depicted as someone who is disappointed with the way that things have turned out, and his actions are fed by greed, as well as by frustration. He reminds me of the truth behind that slightly 'knowing' saying, 'Be careful what you wish for!' In other words, things are not always what we imagine them to be, and even our hopes and dreams, when realised, can cause us significant problems. This is an understatement, of course, in the case of Judas Iscariot, who seemed to be as unclear as to the ultimate outcome of his actions as he was about his motivation for carrying them out.

The crucial moment of the betrayal of Jesus was experienced in the Garden of Gethsemane. This place at the foot of the Mount of Olives, I have felt for a long time as I ponder its significance, is somewhere that we would do well to consider more deeply than we generally do. The events of this late evening; this after supper time, of prayer and challenge in the garden can be lost to our conscious attention amidst the crucial importance of the Last Supper and the swift onward movement to the trial and condemnation of our Lord.

In the Garden of Gethsemane Jesus prayed with his inner band of disciples, Peter, James and John. We know that they could not keep awake; their watch with him was inadequate for those whose role was to be Apostles and leaders of the emerging community of faith. But beyond them, at a short distance was Jesus himself. We are told that Jesus prayed in agony and that his sweat came like great drops of blood falling to the ground, that he was sustained in his prayer and inner struggle by the presence of angels, and that this preparation for meeting his arrest and trial was in some way crucial to all that was to follow.

From our perspective, as onlookers to a scene that is both strange and yet familiar as well, we are left with the sense that feelings of oppressiveness and intensity were nearly crushing Jesus, but the release of the capitulation to the Father's will was what brought the calm control of our Lord in his dealing with the crowd that came out to arrest him. They all knew the place. They passed it every day that they travelled from Bethany (from the home of Lazarus, Martha and Mary) to Jerusalem. It made a good meeting place, very close to the City, but far enough from the crowds to talk and pray in peace. Being there at night would have been different, but the place itself was familiar to them all.

Judas arrives with the soldiers. He is about to book his place in history, and his act is one that has made him the example with which to compare others who seek to betray or undermine the work of another by turning an act of support into one of betrayal. The confrontation of Jesus with the opposition to the Good News he brought had reached its moment of crisis.

Day 38
St John's Gospel, chapter 18, verse 10: 'Then Simon Peter, having a sword, drew it and struck the high priest's slave and cut off his right ear.'

I remember as a child walking home from a violin lesson with 'sixpenny-worth' of chips balanced in a couple of sheets of the *Evening Standard*, or some such, on one of those old violin cases that were like a mini coffin. Approaching me were half a dozen much older girls (of the sort of sporty type immortalised by John Betjeman) intent on teasing this sweet little boy with a violin. Chips went flying, the violin case flew open and everything fell out. I had the presence of mind to pinch one of their rounders bats during the ensuing melee and with my back against a park wall I was ready to defend myself. I was in the classic cornered animal situation. Whatever the odds, however big the threat, never mind the cost, it is human nature to take on a challenge if there seems to be no other way out.

It strikes me that Peter has the same reaction here. He is ready, in the instant and without needing to give it much thought, to take the responsibility of being the second in command and lunging to protect and challenge. He had the sword (albeit, probably a relatively modest large knife or dagger) because they had talked about this earlier. The strike is pathetic in its puny effect upon the opposition, but is in accord with a symbolic channelling of confrontation to bring

Christ to arrest, with the demonstration that this was not a giving of himself into the hands of the high priests, they actually had to get him, use a large show of strength, be devious in utilizing the hours of darkness and the trap of a spy leading them to a special place of meeting. It was a reminder then that this arrest marked a moment of confrontation between good and evil, virtue and underhand dealing, which is borne out not between the High Priest and Jesus, but between the High Priest's slave and the right-hand man to Jesus.

The fact that Jesus heals the slave's ear underlines the fact that the incident is notional and symbolic, rather than being a serious, if futile, attempt to escape the threat of arrest. We are sufficiently familiar with this passage to pass over the obvious point of peculiarity here, namely that they let Peter go. They bound Jesus and arrested him and led him away, but seemed to have lost interest in Peter altogether, even though he was the one who took up arms against them and had actually injured a close associate of the High Priest.

The arrest of Jesus following the intense time of prayer for Jesus and the trying time for the disciples, between desperately trying to stay awake and pray and falling asleep (a condition that I know only too well!) comes as a watershed in the two days that we shall be experiencing at this stage next week, as the reflective support and fellowship of the Upper Room becomes the threatening isolation of the courtyard of the High Priest's house. It is to there we shall be led by St John next.

Day 39
St John's Gospel, chapter 18, verse 17: 'The maid who kept the door said to Peter, "Are you not also one of this man's disciples?" He said, "I am not".'

The Church of Ireland is quite small compared to both the population of Ireland and the Anglican Communion, so it is no surprise that on visiting anywhere, north, south, east or west, in a town or a country church it is not difficult to find some common acquaintance amongst the congregation. 'Are you not so and so?' might easily become, 'You'll know the Reverend this, or Canon that?' Recognition is a great source of comfort for most people – very few are content with absolute anonymity. Connections are a source of conversation, once the subject of the weather has been exhausted!

This little encounter in the courtyard of the High Priest is, of course, of a somewhat different order. This is a challenge, like the questioning of a suspected escapee; and like that situation of interrogation, the questioner is not put at ease with a simple no. Peter is consciously hiding his identity – and it can't be easy – but he wants to be there too and witness what is happening. The precariousness of his situation leads him to deny that he is a disciple of Jesus, a thing he may justify with the thought that there is not much point in being caught and suffering the same fate as Jesus, even if he is only arrested and treated in a less important way. However, the net effect is that he is directly denying his Lord, and this runs counter to his declared position, that he would rather die than fail Jesus.

An identity parade that picks out a face from a group of people has at least a picture in mind of the individual who is searching for a match. In this case it seems as though the terms of recognition are likely to be the general look of someone up from the country in the city, so a bit out of place, plus the fact that others like him had been seen with Jesus – and then, we gather further on, that he speaks like a Galilean too – and dialects and accents are a considerable giveaway.

The crucial point about this for us is that which is made clear in the text itself. Peter is ultimately 'gutted' as we might say in Belfast and brought to see, in no uncertain terms, that he was a failure, through and through. This sad moment for Peter has come to be an occasion of considerable comfort for the rest of us, on the basis that, 'Well, if Peter can deny Jesus three times and managed to be rehabilitated in the eyes of Jesus and for the good of the Church, then there may be hope for me!' As, naturally, there is. Peter failed miserably, but in the end it made him a better apostle and leader for the young Christian Church, that depended so much on the ministry and mission of the closest disciples of Jesus after Pentecost – and, of course St Paul, who made an even worse start to his relationship with Jesus, but ultimately was key to the expansion of the Church in the early days.

Section Seven

Day 40 to Day 47

'Holy Week and Easter'

Day 40 – Palm Sunday
St John's Gospel, chapter 18, verse 20: 'Jesus answered him, "I have spoken openly to the world; I have always taught in synagogues and in the temple, where all Jews come together; I have said nothing secretly".'

On Palm Sunday we begin Holy Week; a week during which we read a great deal of scripture and attempt to expound at least some of it. On Palm Sunday alone, traditionally, there is a reading of the whole story of the Passion of our Lord from one of the Evangelists, but there is an emphasis on the events of Palm Sunday too; Jesus riding into Jerusalem on a donkey, to shouts of hosanna and to the waving palm branches as in this way he arrives in the City of Jerusalem as King. It is a way in which Jesus spoke openly to the world – and he went to the Temple and gave the message there too, that the traders and money changers were out of order, and that the Temple must be seen for what it is: a house of prayer.

I would really like to have a donkey in St Anne's Cathedral on Palm Sunday, but would need to do something to cover the marble floor of the aisle, but the Botanic Gardens in Belfast has traditionally supplied the Cathedral with Palm branches – for which I am very grateful – so we do have a real sense of occasion, even with those. The whole original Palm Sunday story is so sensual: the sight of the waving branches, the sound of the crowd shouting, the touch of palm and cloth and the course hair of the donkey; there would be dust and sunshine, movement, and a great atmosphere of anticipation and joy and expectation. Do you remember that wonderful line about the very stones being called upon to cry out had the people failed to do so? But they didn't fail, did they? They cried 'Hosanna' and it was heartfelt and hopeful and right. Even the way that the donkey was found, by the disciples, adds a sense of drama. It was all planned by Jesus and was certainly an example of having 'spoken openly to the world'.

The fact that the crowd was swayed so rapidly over the course of a few days to reach the point of shouting 'crucify him' of Jesus and calling for the release of Barabbas suggests that we are dealing with a different crowd here on Palm Sunday, to that orchestrated by the religious authorities during the trial before Pilate. Today, social media, the mobile phone, the press and TV and Radio would all play their part in the context of anyone 'speaking openly to the world', once such a person achieves celebrity status. Yet, even in our Lord's day, the word that stirred men and women to action could spread very quickly.

In our own time, the message that the Church brings to the world is always at risk of being lost in the barrage of gossip and news items. Sport, and especially football, has achieved almost the status of a religion. So, whilst the Church seeks to proclaim the words of Christ openly, it can feel that we are doing it in secret as the attention of the world around us is taken up with other things. The week ahead may help us reflect further on the mission that lies at the heart of our Christian discipleship.

Day 41 – The Monday of Holy Week
St John's Gospel, chapter 18, verse 33: 'Pilate entered
the praetorium again and called Jesus, and said to him,
"Are you the King of the Jews?"'

In walking the *via dolorosa* through the ancient streets of the old city of Jerusalem, pilgrims start at two churches which are situated together in one courtyard off the main bustling narrow street, full of pilgrims and traders, children from the nearby school and traffic – everything from hand carts to a Mercedes; from military jeeps to bikes (both pedal and powered), with drivers that seem little concerned for what the devout follower of the Way of the Cross is about.

The churches in this courtyard, which itself can be a place buzzing with hundreds of jostling pilgrims ready to begin this walk to Calvary, mark where Jesus was condemned and flogged. It is here that in prayer and hymn each individual tries to catch the mood of the moment. It is the small things, only too often, which attract our attention when our nerves are at their tautest, or our sensitivities heightened by anticipation and expectation. The sight of the original pavement of the place of judgement, the realisation that the hustling crowd and noise and smell is right; it is authentic to the place and to the reality of this experience. They may be twenty-first-century noises and the pressing crowd in jeans and trainers, as much as anything, but what we experience at that place in the midday sun (or even in heavy rain, as I once walked it) is to be experienced with the distractions and confusion of a market, not in the quiet peace of a retreat.

When Pilate was left to consider the case of Jesus, he did so as one who was under pressure too. He could not block out either the crowd or the leaders of the Jews, who were trying to persuade him to take the action that suited them, by persuading him that it was in his interests too. Self-justification is one of our sources of comfort in the face of taking difficult decisions that should be entirely objective. To try and avoid the position that makes things awkward for us, we can find ourselves arguing for the solution that suits us with all the strength we can muster. This is what Pilate sought: a way out that would satisfy both the religious authorities and himself, whilst trying to release Jesus as well. To have Jesus condemned, but then released (under the 'one prisoner set free at the Passover' tradition) was the ideal outcome from his point of view, but was clearly not acceptable as the crowd was prepared to have a murderer released in preference, so Pilate tried to see if Jesus would condemn himself from his own mouth.

Jesus is pressed by Pilate to admit that he claimed to be the King of the Jews, or at least a king anyway, and this discussion with our Lord occupies the next few verses, and ends with the verse in which Pilate asks, 'What is truth?' that we shall consider tomorrow. It is enough for now to recognise the dangers of compromising oneself in the face of pressure; Peter has already done this to his horror and shame, but Jesus, as always, just finds the right words; he answers calmly, without threat, but with immense authority, indicating quite clearly that he was, and indeed is, Christ the King.

Day 42 – The Tuesday of Holy Week
St John's Gospel, chapter 18, verse 38a: 'Pilate said to him, "What is truth?"'

There is an incident in one of the Richmal Crompton *Just William* books in which William Brown, that rather cynical observer of adult behaviour, decides (I think on hearing a Christmas Day sermon in Church) that he must change his ways to a path of utter truthfulness. No matter what the cost to him, he will be completely truthful. The beginning of his campaign – rather unfortunately – is his reflection on his Christmas presents and on family members assembled to share the day together. Polite acceptance is no longer an option; the newly truthful pattern that must be followed, by William, was to be adopted with rigid application. He subsequently manages to offend most of the family and visitors – with the net effect that he is not entirely sure that adults are really interested in the truth, however they may entreat children to be truthful.

This may not appear to have much relevance in relation to the text before us today, relating to Pilate's inner struggle with his conscience. What it does in fact do is to demonstrate that a lot of what we treat as truth in daily life is not by any means absolute. Truth may be expressed in words that change their meaning according to the expression used by the speaker, with the use of irony and sarcasm, by turning a statement into a question, by placing a parenthesis in the sentence or more tellingly, by adding inverted commas. Pilate appears to have this flexible understanding of truth and cannot really understand our Lord's words when he speaks of bearing 'witness to the truth' (verse 37).

Truth for Jesus is an uncomplicated, absolute value, that is not only something he speaks, but more obviously he personifies – he *is* the truth. Jesus reflects, in chapter 14, that he is 'the way, the truth, and the life'. These are all absolute qualities when considered from the theological angle; this meaning being underlined by the authority of Christ himself. Yet Pilate treats them, or at least the word 'truth' as if it held the natural flexibility of the theoretical; allowing a range of interpretations according to context. Truth is certainly an abstract concept which he can treat dismissively; at one step removed from what he is actually forced to do. So, his use of the word here in a metaphorical sense to try and demonstrate that, whilst he wishes to be seen to have striven for what he understands to be the truth, he fails in the face of the united opposition that has been assembled for the day.

It is at this point that one can detect the growing impatience of Pilate. He wants to release Jesus. He probably realises that he is harmless, but, he cannot afford to look weak either. Yet his attempt to have Jesus released under the tradition of releasing one prisoner at the Passover was never likely to work; for Jesus, in the eyes of the High Priest, must die. The truth of the matter lay entirely in the person of Jesus himself, and that truth Pilate had rejected, openly and finally, as Jesus is condemned to scourging, mockery and crucifixion.

Day 43 – The Wednesday of Holy Week
St John's Gospel, chapter 19, verse 6: 'When the chief priests and the officers saw him, they cried out, "Crucify him, crucify him!" Pilate said to them, "take him yourself and crucify him, for I find no crime in him."'

The impatience that was revealed in the text 'What is truth?' (which we considered yesterday) spills over from his utterance, 'Behold the man!' or 'Here is the man!' of chapter 19, verse 5 with a sense of exasperation and I suspect an element of sarcasm. This offhand 'you cannot be serious!' approach to Jesus (with, one would have to say, the niggling element of doubt) is not shared by the chief priests. They have an entirely different agenda. They have started down a path to eliminate Jesus and are not going to be thwarted at this point.

The Wednesday in Holy Week is still in a quiet period of the week for many parishes. Some will have services every day; others may concentrate on Maundy Thursday and Good Friday. From the perspective of a daily reading for an individual, we can do a lot worse than consider this text before us, for, though liturgically we have not yet reached the Last Supper, in our minds at this stage of Holy Week the crucial elements leading to the arrest, trial and crucifixion of Jesus are all in place. We have a day to consider how we can attempt to absorb the whole of what we are about to read and hear, between now and Good Friday, that will help us to understand and enter-into the Passion of Christ.

The chief priests and the officers are crying, 'Crucify him!' Pilate is reaching the end of his tether and is ready to capitulate to their demands; the disciples appear to have disappeared altogether. What are they doing? Why does not one of the Evangelists tell us? So here we are. Preachers are half way through their series of addresses for Holy Week, the Flower Guild are planning the church decorations for Easter, the choir is summoning itself for the next few days, and all of us need a break to pause and think and pray. Would we be with the chief priests, or beside Pilate, or hidden – who knows where? It is time to enter in thought and prayer, to try and share this time with others across the Church and feel ourselves to be in the places, and with the people, that we shall visit in the next forty-eight hours – The Upper Room, Gethsemane, the High Priest's House, Pilate, Herod and Calvary.

Visualising a location (that we achieve with the imagination) is not everyone's approach to the stories of the Bible, but I have found it to be helpful in trying to understand the way that both the followers of Jesus, and those who oppose him, seek to act. One needs quiet and undistracted time, the scriptures – and in this case the Gospels – open, and the patience and discipline to read, and pause, and return to the text, taking a small piece at a time. Try to live each moment.

Day 44 – Maundy Thursday
St John's Gospel, chapter 19, verse 26: 'When Jesus saw his mother, and the disciple whom he loved standing near, he said to his mother, "Woman, behold, your son!" Then he said to the disciple, "Behold, your mother!"'

Today, Maundy Thursday, is a day of complex relationships being revealed at the edge of the conscious awareness of those closest to Jesus. The moment at the Cross, revealed in the text that I have chosen for today, is similarly on that edge of conscious awareness, where love and pain and loss find their expression in words and actions.

There are moments in all of our lives when these things come together, with the lasting effect of gouging out a deeply scored memory that will be with us forever. Some people live with horrendous burdens of guilt or sorrow, many are held in the prayers and shared support of others, and all of these matters which bring light into the dark place of loss, show that human beings can know Christ on the cusp of their deepest needs.

Jesus and his disciples are seen by the Church in two locations today: the Upper Room for the Last Supper, including the incident of Jesus washing the disciples' feet, and the Garden of Gethsemane, which holds in its oppressive shade the agony of Christ's prayers and the clamour of his arrest. On the surface, there is little to alleviate the gloom as the seriousness of the atmosphere at the Last Supper, including the mysterious departure of Judas, transfers to the sleepy inattention of the inner group of the disciples in the olive grove of Gethsemane.

But, through all of this there is a discernable thread that we are following. It traces through the tensions of these hours the loving and understanding presence of Jesus in our midst. As our Lord takes a towel and washes his disciples' feet, he is demonstrating the ministry of the servant that is part of the Christian calling, but he is also entering the mind of the disciples in a new way; he particularly challenges Peter over this act. Jesus is able to live with the paradox that stretches us, which John declares in his Gospel account. He can be Lord and servant, he can teach his disciples through the physicality of the sharing of a meal and on another occasion proclaim the sufficiency of the Spirit compared to the weakness of 'the flesh'. There is no separation – the person of Jesus is one who can offer his own life for that of the world, whilst bringing comfort, forgiveness and strength to individuals through expending his dying breaths on Mary and John.

I have long felt that Gethsemane holds the clue to more than we often see in that Garden. It is there that the struggle in Christ's heart reaches its climax; it is there that the relative strength of our Lord to his disciples is revealed in its fullness: Jesus bearing the cup of the world's sin; Peter, James and John struggling to keep awake. There is something that is taut to the point of breaking about this evening gathering at the foot of the Mount of Olives. Here we find our place as those in need; here our struggles are seen in the wider context of the world's grief; here too we know the personal care that Jesus holds for every one of us – and he gives his life for us all.

Day 45 – Good Friday
St John's Gospel, chapter 19, verse 30: 'When Jesus had received the vinegar, he said, "It is finished" and he bowed his head and gave up his spirit.'

Every Good Friday, some people will spend three hours in Church meditating on Christ's seven words from the Cross, the sixth of these seven words is that spoken by Jesus in the text for today: 'It is finished.' As the darkening sky of which Matthew, Mark and Luke speak reflected the symbolic importance of what was being witnessed, as the hours of which Jesus hung on the Cross come to an end.

On a visit to Oberammergau to see the Passion Play in the year 2000, we watched the performance in increasing gloom – bear in mind the stage is open to the elements. The actor playing Jesus was raised upon the cross, high into the air and the thieves on either side. As the play continued, the threat of a storm increased until at last as we watched the final part of the crucifixion there was thunder and forked lightning against the darkened afternoon sky. We asked ourselves silly questions like, 'How could the producers of the play manage this?' Then, pinching ourselves, we realised that this was no film being portrayed on a large screen, it was a live play and the lightning and thunder, some-how coincidental to what was being acted out. Or was it? Believe me it was enough to raise the hairs on the back of one's neck.

But what is it that we learn from this word? Simply believing that the work of redemption was achieved by Christ on the Cross is a start. The very fact of faith in the Cross of Christ is a kind of shorthand for the whole of Christian belief. But then comes the response. The importance of the Christian community, the fellowship of believers, the Eucharistic fellowship, of which you and I are a part, is not one entirely parish-based. There is an immediate source of our corporate life around the communion table in every parish church, but the wider sense of being part of the whole people of God is not only important, in the view of the Anglican Communion, it is vital. Hence the support for ecumenical ventures as well as the larger picture of life in the Diocese and throughout Ireland, seeing the Church as wider than any one tradition.

So it is that the Church is not just an institution, but more fundamentally it is a body, a community with which Christ has entrusted his sacramental presence. We may think of it, both in the aspect of the Christ achieving redemption for the world through the shedding of his blood, but also, as he bowed his head in St John's description, he committed the continuance of his work to the community of his followers. But we are not only playing our part in a body, a community of faith, we are also individuals seeking the path of discipleship and, as we see this passing moment of this word from the Cross, marking as it does a finishing and yet a new beginning, let us train our eyes to see the mystery of this passing and renewal in our lives day by day.

The ultimate moment of this passing from life to death was that of the achieving of the Father's purpose on the Cross; so note our Lord's cry, for it is a cry of victory, rather than one of capitulation: 'It is finished.' As he bowed his head in commitment of his life and work into his Father's hands, he also committed his life and work to all who love and serve him in this life, until we lay down our charge for a new generation to take up.

Day 46 – Easter Eve
St John's Gospel, chapter 19, verse 41: 'Now in the place where he was crucified there was a garden, and in the garden a new tomb where no one had ever been laid.'

Easter Eve is, for many people, a day of shopping and preparation for Easter Day and a family gathering, though patterns are changing and some parishes discover that parishioners are away, and the influx of visitors and those who attend only a few times a year to receive communion, are barely balancing, numerically, those regulars who have travelled elsewhere.

Church decorating is another task undertaken on this Saturday. The smell of daffodils and lilies and the sight of the predominantly white and yellow flowers of early Spring is a sign of the new life proclaimed at Easter right across Ireland and Britain. The dramatic change from a barren church on Good Friday to the glories of Easter is a symbolic way of showing what is happening liturgically and, in some measure, within us. I use, 'in some measure' advisedly, for to mentally and spiritually part from Good Friday, with the sorrow of the suffering and death of Jesus, and then to embrace fully the joy of Easter is a transition that is not easy to make in less than forty-eight hours.

Today is a day that helps that process considerably, for it is, liturgically, an interim day. In those parishes holding an Easter Vigil service, with a fire burning brightly outside the main church door – bringing reminiscence of St Patrick and the fire of Easter kindled on the Hill of Tara – before symbolically carrying, as a glowing candle in the gloom, the light of Christ into the church on the eve of the Sunday, there is the reaffirmation of the centrality of the Crucifixion of our Lord, to its miraculous conclusion through reading and prayer and song – to the Resurrection; to what every Christian clings: 'He is risen, Alleluia!'

Christ's body is laid in a tomb, as the Synoptic Gospels record, that had been 'hewn out of the rock'. St John describes it as merely, a 'new tomb' in 'the garden', but emphasises the lavishness of even this, probably temporary, burial: a huge weight of spices, a linen shroud, a private garden and a new tomb. The women were to return after the Sabbath, but in the meantime, the body of Jesus lay in this garden tomb with the amazing event of the Resurrection awaiting a world unprepared for such a miracle.

That sense of expectation that we have on Easter Eve can be imagined, in a slightly different way, when we consider that even at this moment, the disciples and the women, who were with Jesus, had no anticipation that life was about to change for them forever, even though Jesus had warned them! We wait today with prior knowledge of exactly how things were to be and so can be better prepared, but we have still to turn the 'story' of the Resurrection into an actual a heart-changing reality in our thinking and prayer – to know in faith and love, the risen Lord within us. So let us sleep well tonight and be ready to joyfully sing 'Alleluia' tomorrow!

Day 47 – Easter Day
*St John's Gospel, chapter 20, verse 13: 'The angels said
to her, "Woman, why are you weeping?" She said to
them, "Because they have taken away my Lord, and I
do not know where they have laid him".'*

St John gives us the details of the first Easter Day
in eighteen wonderful verses of chapter 20. His
account is particularly emotive as it contains the
grief and anguish of Mary Magdalene. St John
makes us feel her pleading cry, 'They have taken
away my Lord and I do not know where they
have laid him.' She can bear no more, she weeps
helplessly and is in deep distress. John
remembers how he and Peter had left Mary there
– they had seen the empty tomb, and the
impression given to the reader is that they were
in a state of shock; they didn't know what to
think. John writes that they didn't understand
the scripture that he must rise from the dead.
They left Mary to weep alone.

John shows us the constant requirement that
the disciples had for some more evidence; the
evidence of touch, that physical something,
which turned questioning, amazed awe into faith
in a risen and glorified Lord. The touch of
confirmation (Peter and John did not have it and
they 'went back to their homes') helped to bring
reassurance to what they believed with their eyes
when they saw that the tomb was empty, but
could go no further. Mary Magdalene, when her
eyes were opened to Jesus, wanted to hold him.

Thomas later on, wanted to touch the wounds, then he would believe, but John shows that in the end, they were denied that touch – yet still they believed. Thomas refused to touch and Mary Magdalene, equally, just knew; 'I have seen the Lord,' she told the disciples. But let us look again at her encounter with Jesus.

Peter and John left her weeping, perhaps they didn't realise just how distraught she was becoming, perhaps they could not see beyond their own grief, or maybe they had nothing to offer her; they were drained by the previous forty-eight hours and could take no more. What happened next is definitely bound up with those he loves, in sorrow and in joy. Notice the gentle questioning of the angels, 'Woman, why are you weeping?' In John's account, that is all that they say – it is the voice of one trying to console, to gently draw out, to prepare for the encounter that was about to take place – yes, there was a divine presence, not only the angels being there, but in their approach to this grief-stricken young woman. What made Mary turn, we don't know; maybe the shadow of Jesus fell on her from behind, perhaps she heard a footstep, anyhow, she did turn. She saw the risen Lord, but took him to be the gardener; probably she didn't even look up. He too, like the angels asks, 'Why are you weeping?' But he adds, 'for whom are you looking?'

Then occurs the intimate moment of their reunion, and as we read, we are struck by the light and life which is apparent as the wonderful encounter unfolds. But we too must learn, with Mary Magdalene, that love and trust and service, are not dependent on touch, or even sight. The Resurrection marked not so much an end to the caress and touch, but a new beginning which, in the end, was to bring a more profound sense of fuller love and life and union with Christ. The Resurrection of Jesus opens new life for us all. It was *the* thing that the early Church talked and talked about – that their Lord was alive – not in the old way of age and decay, but of a new age, and as a new source of hope and life for us all.

The conditions for the enjoyment of this new life, this eternal life, are essentially simple, though the results of its possession go deep and are far-reaching. 'Anyone who loves me,' Jesus says, 'will heed what I say; then my Father will love him, and we will come and make our dwelling with him.' That union means life – full life, in the here and now – and life that is eternal.

'Because I live,' said Jesus, 'you too, will live.'

Questions for Reflection

Questions for discussion group or individual thought after each succeeding Wednesday following Ash Wednesday, up to and including the week before Holy Week.

Section One – 'The Challenge'

1. What would we expect John the Baptist to say if he were interviewed on radio or television today?

2. What moment can you think of in your life when you really wish you had spoken, but in fact said nothing? What moment do you wish you had stayed silent, but didn't? Why? Would you act differently today?

3. Is there some equivalent of a desert experience, such as John or Jesus would have had, that we might gain in Ireland today? Would you seek it?

4. Why did Jesus turn the water into wine?

5. 'How can a man be born when he is old?'

6. Is the challenge of the appearance of John and the coming of Jesus felt in any aspects of the daily life of Irish people today? What are the opportunities to make such a challenge relevant?

Section Two – 'Concerning Water'

1. Why do people want to be remembered? Is it important for you to leave something behind to ensure you are not forgotten?

2. How can individuals and groups that have become embittered break the cycle of mutual ill will?

3. How would you have responded to the man at the pool of Bethesda before the arrival of Jesus to heal him?

4. Joy is a natural response to the gift of life in, with and for Jesus. How is this borne out in your life?

5. Do you think that the disciples were being tested by Jesus before he fed the five thousand?

6. The symbolism of water in different ways is expressed this week. In reality we may take clean water for granted, but we are aware that access to water in many parts of the world is a major issue for our day and for the future. How can we, in Ireland, do more to help?

Section Three – 'Difficult Questions'

1. Is my witness to Jesus Christ to be measured against the expectations of others?

2. How can the Church be active in eradicating the exploitation of women in our society?

3. If your parish church had to close, how would this affect you?

4. Do you link sin and misfortune?

5. What do you make of Arthur Blessitt and his cross on wheels (day 20)?

6. How should the Church be actively asking (and answering) the 'difficult question' that affect people, not only in Ireland, but internationally?

Section Four – 'Service and Sacrifice'

1. How important is celebration in your life, and to what extent is that part of what you are as a Christian?

2. Are you a Mary or a Martha? Can you be both?

3. The Church is training its lay people and clergy to be leaders. Should ambition be part of that package?

4. During the Olympic Games even very important worldwide events seemed to take second place to the sport. Is this temporary distraction healthy or a serious mistake?

5. How should love be expressed by a Christian community?

6. What are the limits that should be considered for establishing a level of foreign aid for developing countries?

Section Five – 'The Last Supper'

1. How does the peace that Christ offers pass our understanding?

2. Taking any area of division in the world, say Israeli and Palestinian, how would you propose a solution, reflecting on the basis of Christ's teaching on our neighbour?

3. How do you respond to the passing of time? Do we have a healthy understanding in Christianity about aging and care and death?

4. Could you have lived the life of an early Celtic Christian?

5. Is churchgoing a form of seeking sanctuary?

6. Does the fact that not all Christians share in the Eucharist matter for the Church's witness to the world?

Notes

[1] These five sections cease after day 36 (the Wednesday before Palm Sunday) as I am working on the assumption that Lent discussion groups will finish before Holy Week.

[2] Sontag, S., *As Consciousness is Harnessed to Flesh* (Hamish Hamilton, 2012), p. 4.

[3] The place traditionally identified as the baptism site of Jesus. It is marked by a number of Christian Churches. A new Anglican place of worship is to be built soon.

[4] Published by Jonathan Cape, 2011.

[5] Hymn 601 in the Church of Ireland Church Hymnal (5th Edition), OUP, 2000.

[6] 'How deep the Father's love for us' by Stuart Townsend.